The I...
Individual

Michel Syrett & Jean Lammiman

- Fast track route to fostering and managing innovation in the workforce

- Covers the key areas of how ideas are inspired in individuals, from how to shape and test innovative projects and how individuals respond to innovation-based change to how to reward them for their creative output

- Examples and lessons from some of the world's most successful businesses, including the Disney Corporation, BMW, Shiseido and L'Oréal, and ideas from the smartest thinkers including Charles Handy, Gary Hamel, Daniel Goleman and Michael Eisner

- Includes a glossary of key concepts and a comprehensive resources guide.

essential management thinking at your fingertips

Copyright © Capstone Publishing 2002

The right of Michel Syrett and Jean Lammiman to be identified as the authors of this work has been asserted in accordance with the Copyright, Designs and Patents Act 1988

First published 2002 by
Capstone Publishing (a Wiley company)
8 Newtec Place
Magdalen Road
Oxford OX4 1RE
United Kingdom
http://www.capstoneideas.com

CIP catalogue records for this book are available from the British Library and the US Library of Congress

ISBN 1-84112-317-X

Printed and bound in Great Britain

This book is printed on acid-free paper

Contents

Introduction to
ExpressExec

ExpressExec is 3 million words of the latest management thinking compiled into 10 modules. Each module contains 10 individual titles forming a comprehensive resource of current business practice written by leading practitioners in their field. From brand management to balanced scorecard, ExpressExec enables you to grasp the key concepts behind each subject and implement the theory immediately. Each of the 100 titles is available in print and electronic formats.

Through the ExpressExec.com Website you will discover that you can access the complete resource in a number of ways:

» printed books or e-books;
» e-content – PDF or XML (for licensed syndication) adding value to an intranet or Internet site;
» a corporate e-learning/knowledge management solution providing a cost-effective platform for developing skills and sharing knowledge within an organization;
» bespoke delivery – tailored solutions to solve your need.

Why not visit www.expressexec.com and register for free key management briefings, a monthly newsletter and interactive skills checklists. Share your ideas about ExpressExec and your thoughts about business today.

Please contact elound@wiley-capstone.co.uk for more information.

Introduction to the Innovative Individual

- » Difference as normality.
- » The individual as king.
- » Fostering the creative spark.

"The past is a foreign country: they do things differently there."

One of the twentieth century's most poignant novels, *The Go-Between*,[1] started this way. Today the author might have written that tomorrow morning is as much a foreign country as the past. Doing things differently from one day to the next is as bewildering an experience to the individual at the turn of the twenty-first century as analyzing the events of the first half of the last century was to the hero of the novel. It can also breed the same mistrust of life.

Yet doing things differently, as an organization and as an individual, is what twenty-first-century working is all about. When the great business gurus of the 1990s, Gary Hamel and Richard Pascale, wrote that an organization's ability to change is the only capability that really matters, they also meant its ability to innovate.

The dramatic world events that followed the terrorist attacks on New York on September 11 is a vivid illustration of this. At the time of writing (October 2001) it was unclear whether they would help to generate a full-blown recession in 2002 but they have certainly increased the likelihood.

In some industries – most notably airlines and tourism – the out-of-the-blue collapse in consumer confidence it provoked has been overnight and almost without precedent. In the case of one initiative profiled in this title, the design of new working practices at the new headquarters of British Airways (see Chapter 4), the future of the building is currently under review. In another of the cases, IntegriSys (see profile of Angus Friday in Chapter 7), delays in closing key contracts have led to a significant difficulty in raising further venture capital.

Economic uncertainty, however mild and for however short a time, will certainly affect the issues raised in this title. Nortel Networks, one of the world's leading manufacturers of telecommunications technology, recently launched an intellectual property award scheme that rewards employees who successfully register a patent for a new product or service. They did so not only to recognize and reward the work of their scientific and research staff, but to emphasize to the whole workforce the importance of intellectual property to the firm's future. As Nortel's European head of intellectual property, Ewen Bewley, comments: "Ideas are our lifeblood and they come from individuals, not processes or the application of new technology."

But individuals are, well, individual. They respond to change in different ways and have agendas that do not always neatly tie in with those of their employers. While an organization can expect any worker to undertake their work to a consistently high standard, the standards and parameters they work to are laid down for them. Expecting them to stick their neck out to change things is a different matter. If employers want them to go this particular extra mile, they have to start giving serious thought to the circumstances in which they are most likely to do so. One of the most important psychological barriers to creativity in individuals is an uncertainty about their future (see Chapter 6).

If an individual feels their job may be at risk or their future with the organization is uncertain, the incentive to take risk and experiment in their work is bound to be impaired. Job losses and promotion freezes are bound to be a part of any strategy to cut back during an economic slowdown but as Marion Devine's research on mergers and acquisitions (see Chapter 6) and Karen Stephenson's research on organization networks (see Chapter 7) both illustrate, countering rumor with fact and honest feedback can do a lot to prevent a total meltdown in the organization's innovative capability.

Regardless of economic circumstances, organizations should also ask themselves why their staff should bother to be creative anyway. If an individual – whether an assembly line worker or an R&D boffin – has an idea that might transform the company's fortunes, then he or she is sitting on a negotiable asset.

Putting it at its bluntest, the individual has it and the organization hasn't. The individual might need the organization's resources to make it reality but he or she can just as easily turn to another firm or even raise the necessary resources personally, with a bigger payback for him or her self.

This turns the conventional relationship between the individual and the organization on its head. If organizations want to tap the innovative potential of their staff, then they have to provide an environment and a set of motivations that will foster and support this potential.

Conventional command and control systems bury creativity. The very words presuppose new ideas can be summoned up to order. Moreover, they presuppose that ideas only come from certain parts of the organization – the board, the R&D department, the senior management team – rather than the whole workforce.

The high salaries paid to senior managers are justified, in their eyes and that of the organization, by the fact that they are paid to "know it all." Invert the triangle and say, as leading management thinkers are now saying, that the job of the workers is to provide the ideas that make the future and the job of managers is to foster and support these, and you are suddenly dealing with very frightened people. Little wonder that the task of championing the ideas of others is still not an accepted management priority. Yet it can and must be.

Whatever the immediate consequences of the war against international terrorism, the borders of those few remaining countries in the developed world that have not engaged in global trade are fast being eroded. These physical boundaries are being rendered meaningless anyway, by a growth in e-commerce that will soon overcome the recent crash of dotcom companies on the international stock markets. Taking advantage of immediate access to customers around the world requires a knowledge and insight that cannot be encompassed by one person or a single management team at the top of the organization. That knowledge resides in the people doing the trade, whether this is across a counter, through a call center, or sitting at a computer terminal.

Yet while commerce has moved on, and the emerging philosophies from business schools are starting to understand the implications, management practice on the ground is still often stuck in limbo. The innovative individual is king, yet many senior managers do not know it or if they do, do not act on this knowledge.

The intellectual leap they need to make is not great. It is as simple as the comment made by the pioneering chief executive of Scandinavian Airways some 20 years ago:

> "It makes no difference who comes up with the good ideas. All that matters is that the ideas have worked."

NOTES

1 Hartley, L.P. (1954) *The Go-Between*. Alfred Knopf, New York.

What is Meant by the Innovative Individual?

» Personal characteristics.
» Bringing creativity to work or keeping it to yourself.
» The creative as everyman.

The innovative individual – for which also read creative, entre-preneurial, and high-flying – has been a holy grail for employers. And like the real grail, the concept of a distinct, identifiable, recruitable, and retainable group of people that can be labeled "innovative" is part myth and part reality.

EXPLORING THE MYTH

A number of definitions exist of who innovative individuals are, but one of the most insightful was made by Marsha Sinetar, a researcher at the Massachusetts Institute of Technology who undertook a study of "creative" staff in the late 1980s. Sinetar's study of hundreds of managers with a track record of successful innovation revealed that they had the following things in common:

» they are easily bored, and would rather move into untried areas;
» they are perfectly comfortable with ambiguous situations;
» they are happy to take risks – and indeed enjoy doing so;
» they are intellectually curious, needing to use their minds to solve difficult, personally fulfilling problems; and
» they often tend to see their work as a calling or dedicated vocation.

Innovative individuals, Sinetar argued, possess personalities that thrive on freedom in three important areas of life: freedom in the general area of their work and the way in which work gets done; freedom to come up with novel or disturbing questions; and freedom to come up with unusual solutions to the things they're currently thinking about, sometimes in the form of what seem, to others, to be impractical ideas.

Yet at the same time, she concluded, these "creatives" are not always easy to spot. With respect to most of the small customs of life, they may be very ordinary, even boring people. This is borne out by experience elsewhere. Art Fry, the scientist who invented Post-It Notes, was a not-very-highly-rated member of 3M's R&D staff who was working on a failed adhesive project – the very failure of which prompted Fry to think of other ways they could use the stuff.

Gwilym Rees-Jones, the manager at British Airways who revolution-ized work methods at the company's new Waterside headquarters (see Chapter 6), is at first sight indistinguishable in the phalanx of gray suits that litter the corporation's corridors. The organization development advisor who implemented his ideas had no idea who he was when she sat next to him on a company transit bus one afternoon and when he told her, she was staggered by his unprepossessing appearance and manner. Asked what it was that enabled him to pioneer BA's better use of serendipitous working, hot-desking, and cross-boundary thinking, he replied: "stubbornness."

STUBBORNNESS AND A SINGLE MIND

Therein lies the biggest clue to understanding the innovative individual. Once they are convinced they are right, there is no gainsaying them. They dig in for the duration.

Sinetar's research suggests that innovators often make rotten team members. They can alienate colleagues by an intensive and almost obsessive focus on what others see as pet projects or idiosyncrasies, and often see management activities as uninteresting and irritating; or, as in the case of Rees-Jones, they conform in every outward way to management norms, but quietly beaver away to achieve the breakthrough they want through less dramatic subversion. What unites the idiosyncratic loner and the quiet subversive is a stubborn refusal to give in. One such type told us: "I do not break rules, I ignore them."

One thing that becomes very clear from all the studies is that innovative individuals crop up anywhere. Companies that make systematic use of suggestion boxes or competitions – as do Hewlett-Packard, Toyota, and shipbuilders Kvaerner – find that many of the best ideas come from front-liners – managers or assembly workers – who have no predisposition to creativity but can spot solutions that R&D staff cannot.

At Kvaerner, for instance, the company made savings of $45,000 per annum from a suggestion on how to automate the welding of a key component on their assembly line – an idea that originated from welder Arne Svennson. And a simple suggestion for an alteration to Kvaerner's Pulping Recovery Boiler (changing the boiler's base from a rectangle to an octagon) has made the unit cheaper and 15% more efficient. It was proposed by an administrator, Andres Palmergon.

Other organizations have found that whether an individual is disposed to be creative on their employer's behalf depends on whether they are motivated to be so. In the early 1990s, British Petroleum conducted a series of career development workshops for managers deemed to be "plateaued" or blocked in their promotion prospects. During the course of a series of questions about their outside interests and pastimes, it emerged that these individuals had highly creative lives. They were school governors, local politicians, active in the community, or amateur experts in particular fields. Some helped their spouses to run home-based businesses. Further questioning revealed that these activities had given them insights and perspectives that were easily transferable to their mainstream work, yet such transfers didn't occur because the managers were not minded to do so. They were creative enough to find ways of making a difference in their personal lives, but they did not feel it was worth taking this creativity into work.

And here is where the myth about "the innovative individual" starts to kick in. It is the old "nurture or nature?" debate. Is creativity, like leadership, something that people are born with? Or do the kernels of creativity lie in us all, waiting to be teased out by an employer insightful enough to provide the right motivation and environment in which it can flourish?

THE EVERYMAN VIEW

The legendary Michael Eisner, who turned around Disney in the 1990s, commented in a recent interview for *Harvard Business Review*:

> "Ideas come from anywhere. Many of us come up with ideas driving to work, walking around the house, watching our kids at sporting events, everywhere ... (but) good ideas have a habit of getting lost. They fall through the cracks, or they get mired in bureaucracy, and everyone is busy in their own orbit. So I nudge. Sometimes all that good ideas or good people need is an advocate who won't shut up."

Employers, or business commentators, have not always taken such an "everyman" view of who the innovative individual is and where he or she comes from. To see why we have come this far, we need to take a closer look at how management theory has changed over the last two decades.

KEY LEARNING POINTS

» Innovation, for individuals, is often about freedom: freedom in how they work, freedom to ask awkward questions, freedom to come up with unusual solutions to the things they are currently thinking about.

» Innovation is also about being stubborn: not taking no for an answer, not taking the collective or "team" view, and sticking to their own perspective.

» These traits are bred in all of us: whether we feel able to demonstrate them depends on the way we feel about the organization and the environment in which we work.

The Evolution of the Innovative Individual

» The individual and the organization in business history.
» Taylorism and the science of management: the individual subordinate to process.
» Deming and Juran: the individual as the proponent of quality.
» Handy and Mintzberg: the individual as the victim and beneficiary of change.
» Hamel and Pascale: the individual as the source of innovation.

To understand the revolution in thinking that has taken place regarding the innovative individual, you have to focus on the word "individual" before you start trying to define the word "innovative." During the second half of the twentieth century, thinking about organizations changed, from seeing them as machines with working parts that need to be maintained and upgraded, to the ideas that they are living organisms that behave collectively like any other "complex adaptive system" on the planet and around it.

This wider debate about the nature of the organization is covered elsewhere in the ExpressExec series (see *Change Management* and *Organizational Behavior*). But we need to revisit some of the issues, because attitudes regarding who is innovative and in what circumstances go hand in hand with how senior managers see the organization as a whole.

QUAKER CONFORMITY

Everything starts with Taylor. F.W. Taylor was a Pittsburgh Quaker engineer who invented "scientific management" at the turn of the twentieth century. Taylor's approach, seeking maximum efficiency by breaking down tasks into separate movements and finding the one best way of performing each, was the basis for Henry Ford's mass-production revolution.

Taylor's work became the basis of the work-study and time-and-motion studies of the 1920s and 1930s, and subsequently the foundation of the management philosophy of the US Army during World War II. He often used the analogy of baseball, where every element is broken down and studied by coaches before the most effective method of performing each movement is drilled into the team.

Note the word "drilled." The role of the individual in Taylorist management culture is to perform each task or movement to his or her best ability. Taylor was the first to emphasize, in his work *Scientific Management*,[1] that management should study each worker for "his possibilities for development." But the context in which this development takes place is calculated entirely by higher scientific study. The individual lacks the objective perspective or scientific knowledge to judge whether the process in hand is best suited to the job.

The problem with the Taylorist view of things – and Robert Waterman (one of the authors of *In Search of Excellence*[2]) believes that many managers are still Taylorists at heart – is that it does not adapt well to rapidly changing circumstances. The consequences, both good and bad, were demonstrated vividly in the European theater of World War II when a US (and, to a lesser extent, British) army which had been created at very short notice on Taylorist principles came up against a German army organized along very different lines. The best officers in the US army chose to enter the branches of service in which the Taylorist preconditions – a stable environment where problems could be solved through scientific assessment and calculation – already existed: staff work, logistics, and heavy artillery that operated from well behind the lines. The result was that, during the course of the 1943–5 campaigns, the US army was consistently the best supplied and supported force in the entire conflict.

On the front line, things were very different. The German army placed a high premium on flexible, small-scale teamwork, with initiative being devolved to junior officers and NCOs rather than field commanders, who were so employed by the US and British armies. Troops were organized into hastily improvised "battle groups" that could form and re-form under different circumstances, rather than the rigid battalions and brigades of the Allied armies. The result was that consistently, from the first to the last battles, German front-line formations ran rings around US formations, where soldiers and junior officers had not been taught to use their initiative – only to be pulverized by centrally-coordinated US air and artillery fire organized along Taylorist lines and starved by inferior logistics.

QUALITY AND THE INDIVIDUAL

The shortcomings of Taylorism that were highlighted by the war led to a renaissance in management thinking. Ironically, it initially came not from America, but from war-devastated Japan, although it was instigated in that country by an American statistician, W. Edwards Deming. Total quality management (TQM) was not focused entirely on the individual, but one key element – that planning, production and service should be subject to continuous improvement – required a far higher level of involvement from each member of the whole workforce.

When TQM broke down, as it often did, it was usually because senior management failed to support or act on the initiative it sought to promote in the workforce. As Deming himself wrote: "Faced with problems of people . . . management, in my experience go into a state of paralysis, taking refuge in [the] formation of quality circles and employee or participation groups. These groups predictably disintegrate within a few months from frustration, finding themselves unwilling parties to a cruel hoax, unable to accomplish anything, for the simple reason that no one in management will take on suggestions for improvement."

Part of the problem, from the point of view of individual initiative (for which read innovation) is that the impetus for improvement in TQM is still expected to come from the top of the organization. Initiatives may emerge from lower down but they still have to be endorsed by the board and then "cascaded" down through the organization layer by layer. Under this cascade method, which became a stock in trade for the myriad consultants implementing TQM initiatives in the 1980s, senior managers had to "buy in" before the initiative could be taken to middle managers, middle managers had to "buy in" before the initiative could be taken to junior managers, and so on. The front-line cynicism that emerged from this endless succession of top-down reforms – portrayed so vividly in the Dilbert cartoons (see below) – endures to this day.

CHANGE AND THE LEADERSHIP REVOLUTION

The real breakthrough in the road towards recognizing the true value of individual innovation was the recession at the end of the 1980s, which finally brought to an end the post-war era of stability and complacency. In the rethink that occurred during the recovery, the change management movement was born – and the move towards viewing an organization as a collection of individuals bound by a common culture, rather than a machine held together by a series of processes, was made almost overnight.

Early change management thinkers, such as America's John Kotter and Warren Bennis and Britain's Charles Handy, stressed the importance of values-based leadership. This was helped along in great measure by the emergence of a new stable of young entrepreneurs such as The Body Shop's Anita Roddick and the "raspberry rebel" ice cream makers Ben & Jerry, who had grown up in the 1960s and placed staff involvement and enthusiasm at the heart of their business strategy.

Speaking at a conference in Dublin in 1987, for example, Charles Handy commented:

> "The new language of organizations is different. The talk today is of networks and alliances, of "adhocracy" and federalism, of shared values, cultures and consensus. The key words are options not plans, the possible rather than the perfect, involvement instead of compliance. These are the words of political systems not of engineering, they are the language of leadership, not management."

Similarly, John Kotter at a lecture in Harvard Business School argued that change and effective leadership went hand in hand.

> "Major transformations to the organization – to respond to faster technological change, greater international competition and the deregulation of markets – are more and more necessary for them to survive. More change always demands more leadership.
>
> "Consider a simple military analogy. A peacetime army can usually survive with good administration and management up and down the hierarchy, coupled with good leadership concentrated at the very top. A wartime army, however, needs competent leadership at all levels. No one has figured out how to manage people effectively into battle; they must be **led**."

It is very noticeable, however, that at this point in the organization's relationship with the individual, the individual has very little input. He or she responds to the initiative of the "transformational" leader. The leader may need to win the loyalty and enthusiasm of the workforce, and to do so through consultation and by listening to feedback; but in the era of the creative entrepreneur – of Roddick, Branson, Welch, and Eisner – it is *his or her* vision, values, or strategy to which they are responding.

GOING BACKWARDS TO GO FORWARDS

To get to the stage we have reached today – where the individual provides the creativity and the organization responds – the world had to go through another upheaval. In the early 1990s the developed world was going through another recession. With cost efficiency once again on the boardroom agenda, senior managers began to examine ways in which they could achieve greater output for the same investment in resources.

Two pieces of academic work gave them what they thought was the answer: a study of what was termed "lean production," based on work with Toyota and other leading Japanese car manufacturers by a team of researchers from the Massachusetts Institute of Technology; and a new way of designing or "re-engineering" essential business processes, developed by an academic mathematician from the same university called Michael Hammer.

The take-up of business process re-engineering (BPR) was extraordinary. A study by the Economist Intelligence Unit (EIU) in 1993 suggested there had been a 90% take-up. But the immediate savings brought about by the design of more efficient processes were offset by the collapse in morale and loyalty caused by the accompanying job cuts. What particularly incensed individuals was that, out of blind adherence to the precepts of BPR, organizations were making cutbacks in circumstances that did not justify them.

In the US, General Electric led the way, removing 104,000 of its 402,000 workers in 1980–90 even though it faced no great crisis. Compaq cut its workforce by 10% in 1992, despite healthy returns, because it thought the computer industry was bound to stay intensively competitive. Goldman Sachs cut its workforce by 10% in the early 1990s not once but twice – supposedly to increase productivity. Procter & Gamble sent away 13,000 workers even though it was the best performing company in the US in 1992 in its own business sector.

Of course the inventors of lean working and BPR had never intended that their management theories should be used as a figleaf to justify this level of delayering and this volume of redundancies. Both protested in later years that the concepts had been misapplied. But as the US entered the longest period of continued growth in the mid-1990s, the damage had been done.

A new breed of young workers, branded Generation X, had entered the workforce with few illusions about organizations' promises of security and loyalty. The workers that survived were disillusioned and bitter. The Dilbert books of S. Adams, the US cartoonist of daily office life who savagely lampooned the notions of "empowerment" and "employability" that were fashionable at the time, have since become management bestsellers.

More than any other factor, the backlash against BPR – even Hammer admitted that it had clocked up a staggering 70% failure rate in the period 1991-7 – discredited the carefully manufactured and branded "big ideas" that were pouring out of the business schools and management consultancies at the time. This prompted senior managers to look inside their organization for the innovative capability they needed to survive and prosper in a competitive world.

Underpinning this tendency to consider resolving common management problems with internal solutions is the recognition that it is new ideas and not efficient processes or greater productivity that give organizations their competitive edge. As Professor Michael Porter of Harvard Business School stressed in a presentation in 1997:

"Organizations did well to employ the most up-to-date equipment, information technology, and management techniques to eliminate waste, defects, and delays. They did well to operate as close as they could to the productivity frontier. Improving operational effectiveness is **necessary** to achieving superior profitability. But it is not **sufficient**."

THE INDIVIDUAL COMES OF AGE

At this point, the innovative individual came of age. For the first time, the concept of the business leader changed from someone who provided the solutions to someone who helped their front-line staff to find them. At the same time, the definition of R&D as a function was broadened to encompass the development of ideas that front-line staff had originated as well as the creation of original concepts or products themselves.

According to Ronald Heifetz, Director of the Leadership Education Project at Harvard University's John F. Kennedy School of Government, the work of the "adaptive" leader is to simultaneously free front-line workers from the psychological constraints of unnecessary rules and regulations, while throwing out a series of new goals and challenges that will inspire their creativity. (This is explored in greater detail in Chapter 8.) Our own research, conducted for the UK's Roffey Park Management Institute between 1997 and 2001, confirms this. This included personal interviews with 150 senior managers and directors and a series of in-depth case studies of organizations as diverse as major corporations, international non-government organizations (NGOs), and successful dotcom startups. We found that the problem senior managers now perceive as most limiting is not the lack of good ideas on the ground but the lack of organizational ability to identify and effectively develop them.

Ideas, according to one interviewee, were like "diamonds in the dust," unexploited because managers at all levels were not *mandated* to pick them up, recognize their value, and – to pursue the analogy further – arrange to have them expertly cut and polished. While this happens randomly in many organizations at the discretion of managers who have the insight, motivation, and spare time to engage in the task, there is rarely any system or organizational imperative to make this more than a chance process.

Economic uncertainty makes this role an even greater priority because, as we argue in the Introduction, badly handled employee communications in a rumor mill may well lose the organization some of its best creative talent.

This is where we are today. Most senior managers recognize that their future relies on "the innovative individual" but are still struggling to identify and scrap leadership styles and management processes that impede creativity from occurring on a day-to-day basis. The grail they have been looking for – an identifiable and resourceful set of creative individuals – has been under their noses all this time.

The insight that *everyone* is capable of being creative given the right incentives and working conditions is now well known. But the implications of this, in terms of how organizations are structured and run, are still murky. The next three chapters will explore and highlight the insights and good practice that have emerged through the efforts of both managers and commentators to shed some light on the subject.

KEY LEARNING POINTS

» The past 20 years have seen a revolution in the way organizations are perceived: rather than seeing the organization as a machine to be operated and maintained, the idea has emerged that an organization is an organism whose behavior can only be influenced, not controlled.

» One consequence of this revolution has been a bigger focus on the relationship between the individual and the organization, rather than just on the processes that make the organization work.

» The quality of this relationship – measured in how individuals see, think of, and feel about the organization – is linked directly to their ability or willingness to be creative.

TIMELINE

Table 3.1 shows a timeline of the evolution of the concept of the innovative individual as discussed in this chapter.

NOTES

1 Taylor, F.W. (1947) *Scientific Management*, Harper and Row, New York.
2 Peters, T. & Waterman, R.H. (1982) *In Search Of Excellence*, Harper and Row, New York & London.

Table 3.1 Timeline: The evolution of the innovative individual.

Timescale	Prevalent philosophy	Originator(s)
Early twentieth century	*The individual subordinated to process*: the breakdown of work into tasks and tasks into separate movements in order to foster maximum efficiency	F.W. Taylor Frank and Lillian Gilbreth
World War II	*Taylorism at War*: Allied efficiency in marshaling mass air, sea, and logistical resources is offset by German initiative and teamwork on the front line	
Post-war era	*The individual as the proponent of quality*: total quality management brings with it the need for staff to feel enthusiastic about their work – but the measures and parameters are still determined at the top	W. Edwards Deming Joseph M. Juran
1970s–80s	*The individual as the victim and beneficiary of change*: new change management philosophies emphasize the need for shared values and visions but reduced job security makes it hard for a post-war generation to respond	Charles Handy Warren Bennis Henry Mintzberg
Early 1990s	*The individual disempowered by the re-ascendancy of process*: notions of empowerment and employability are discredited by excessive delayering and an accompanying overloading of jobs as employers misinterpret or misapply business process re-engineering or lean production	Rosabeth Moss Kanter Michael Hammer James Womack
Late 1990s	*The individual as the source of innovation*: a new emphasis on innovation stresses the need for a bottom-up approach, with managers facilitating rather than dictating the right way forward, and black and white thinking replaced by a more flexible mindset based on emotional rather than intellectual intelligence	Gary Hamel Richard Pascale Daniel Goleman Michel Syrett and Jean Lammiman

The E-Dimension of the Innovative Individual

» Capturing thought at source.
» Comfort and discomfort with the technology.
» Case study: e-mail as a creative source in a humanitarian crisis.
» Case study: e-mail breaking down barriers in a large corporation.

There probably is no more complex issue concerning the e-mail and Internet revolution than its real – as opposed to theoretical – impact on the creative interactions at work.

CAPTURING THOUGHT AT SOURCE

In theory, e-mail is the biggest thing that has happened to creativity at work since the telephone. It enables individuals to capture their thoughts instantly in text, thus capturing the spontaneity of a face-to-face exchange with the validation that occurs when we see our ideas in print.

Since creative breakthroughs nearly always occur in quick-fire exchanges where the individual does not have the time or need to censor what he or she is saying (see the title *Creativity* in this series and Chapter 6 of this book), e-mail has the capacity to make brain-storming virtual, greatly extending the creative reach of a multisite or multinational organization.

Indeed there is considerable research evidence that brainstorms conducted by e-mail or over the Internet are more productive. Recent tests of new software designed to support electronic brainstorming, involving 800 researchers at the Massachusetts Institute of Technology, found that the creative output from electronic brainstorming sessions was greater than those conducted face-to-face, and furthermore, these productivity gains increased along with the size of group. This was because in face-to-face sessions, the most assertive and outgoing members of the group dominated the exchange, with quieter but equally insightful individuals keeping their thoughts to themselves.

In practice, however, e-mail's capacity to free up thought in the organization depends on two interrelated factors: the extent to which individuals feel comfortable with e-mail and the Internet as a creative medium, and the way exchanges are monitored or regulated by the organization.

A survey of young people by the Economist Intelligence Unit, published in the *Economist* in January 2001, pinpointed a number of ways in which they differed from their older colleagues in the workplace. Among the many contrasts, explored in more detail in this book and also in the ExpressExec title *Creativity*, is a greater ability to learn and relearn faster, to take risks, to combine play with work, and – to a much greater extent than previous generations – to mix or combine personal and work behavior.

The comfort factor

The greatest contrast found by the EIU was in the new generation's ability to take technological change for granted and to feel totally at ease with electronically-based relationships. Our own research confirms much of this. Many of the organizations we studied discovered serious fault lines in their workers' "comfort factor" with new technology. But it was not always a matter of the young versus the old. It was also influenced by the task of the work unit and the way it worked.

British Airways, for example (see case study below), found that the departments that responded best to hot-desking arrangements at their new Waterside headquarters at London's Heathrow Airport were often those that conducted business "on the hop" – a good example being the relationship marketing department where communications with clients were often in transit or offsite. By contrast, the departments in which members spent much more time working at their desks, such as the finance and legal units, were more territorial and less likely to use e-mail or mobile phones for creative work.

The fault lines we discovered cut across several divides. The people least comfortable with e-mail were much less likely to "bond" over the Internet unless they already knew the individual at the other end of the terminal fairly intimately. This also applies to other forms of electronic communication like video conferencing, where the tacit and tactile language that takes place in face-to-face meetings is inhibited or cut off altogether.

In the run up to its merger with Guinness in 1997, for example, the international foods and drinks company Grand Metropolitan (Grand-Met) set up a global taskforce to explore ways in which it could better target emerging economies in Eastern Europe and South East Asia. Members were drawn from around the globe and many of the discussions were conducted through video conferencing. These interchanges were productive but only if they were combined with occasional face-to-face meetings to seal the bond. As the HR director responsible for the interchanges comments:

"You do not feel like you are touching or feeling the person on the screen. There is less gut feel and the whole thing is more process oriented. While this is good in one sense, the fast-wheeling wit and mindplay that can often foster more creative solutions is less easy to achieve."

The intimacy factor also affects the way language is used on the Internet. People less comfortable with electronic communication tend to e-mail or "text" (using mobile phones) the way they write – with all the mental censuring and filtering that goes on when any of us formally composes a letter or report for public consumption. New Agers, on the other hand, e-mail and "text" the way they think. They see electronic communication as a personal interaction in the way older colleagues think of a private phone conversation; and they are much less likely to think twice before committing their thoughts to the screen. Consequently it is far easier, in an interactive exchange with one or more people, to capture the fast-wheeling wit and mindplay that was so visibly lacking in the GrandMet video interchange.

Humanitarianism as a virtual force

We saw this contrast most vividly while, as part of a study on how ideas are shaped in organizations, we monitored Save the Children's action to ward off the potential humanitarian crisis that occurred during the early summer months of 2000, when a second war broke out between Eritrea and Ethiopia, threatening tens of thousands of refugees who were dispersed from their temporary camps by the fighting.

Save the Children's fast response to the crisis, which won it plaudits from the World Health Organization and the Eritrean government, was made possible by e-mail. The essential field infrastructures of non-government organizations (NGOs) are centered around people with the right local knowledge and expertise, supported by easily transportable equipment rather than around buildings and complex technology that may need to be abandoned in a hurry or could be damaged in a bombing raid. These local officers *are* the organization on the ground. Theirs are the decisions that count, because they are the only staff close enough to the situation to keep track of events that may change day by day or even hour by hour.

This was certainly the case in Eritrea. Initial reports stating that the Ethiopian offensive had been contained, and that the refugee camps behind the lines were safe, proved false. Local program officer Bruce MacInnes, sensing this was the case, took a number of key decisions well ahead of time that ensured that Save the Children had the transport and the funds it needed to set up and resource new facilities closer to the capital in order to feed children and vulnerable mothers displaced by the crisis.

E-mail played a critical role in helping MacInnes gain the backing of his organization's regional and international headquarters and in sending emergency appeals to potential donors. For much of the time he was operating from a tiny office in the capital, Asmara, with minimal staff increasingly whittled down by repatriations and, at one point, by local arrests. Most of the initiatives he launched were discussed, reviewed, and resourced through interchanges over the Internet.

E-mail was particularly important in three respects:

» As a source of expert advice. Decisions taken by front-line officers in NGOs are shaped and supported by a team of health and nutritional experts dispersed across a number of countries. In addition, while fundraisers in NGOs are engaged in an aggressively competitive war for donations, the experts share information openly and enthusiastically. Decisions have to be taken in days and sometimes hours, or people die. E-mail means that within minutes of a program officer such as MacInnes coming up with an inspired idea for coping with the crisis, quick-fire exchanges are occurring between opposite numbers, both inside and outside the organization.
» As a source of personal support. Reading through the hundreds of e-mail messages that passed between MacInnes and the London headquarters of Save the Children during the six weeks of the crisis, the weight on his shoulders was very evident. His e-mail is peppered with journalistic descriptions of the suffering caused by the war. He concluded that:

"In the aftermath, the countryside will have bombed villages, razed homes, fields with land mines and unexploded ordnance and traumatized families, coping with the loss of loved ones."

After his assistant was repatriated for safety reasons, he was left with no one to share with. He therefore used e-mail reports to London as a safe way to let off steam and in return, receive messages from distantly-located staff who were "there" for him.

One officer in particular, Sarah Uppard, had worked closely with MacInnes earlier in his career. Their exchanges by e-mail between London and Asmara were packed with a constant stream of informal encouragement, such as "I see you are faced with another emergency! Poor you – hope it goes okay" or (when he had succeeded in raising funds for another expatriate officer) "Gosh, you are on the ball . . . If only I had a little cloning factory turning out people!"

» MacInnes' role as an outposted source of all key decisions in the crisis led to a marked contrast in the way he and his colleagues used e-mail. His London colleagues used the technology as a medium for classic (though highly devolved) communication and control. He, in addition, used e-mail to share personal thoughts and frustrations in a way that would have been either too offensive or too costly using the telex or the phone. "Bruce wears his heart on his sleeve," says regional director Peter Hawkins. "If he thinks f**k, he writes f**k."

The Orwell factor

The very ease and speed of communication of e-mail has, in fact, provoked a highly touchy internal cultural issue at Save the Children. Until its introduction, local programs officers like MacInnes were lords of their own manor – rather like expatriate managers running local officers for big oil or construction firms in the 1950s. E-mail has enabled regional or international directors to keep a closer eye on the day-to-day activities of local officers in a way that they sometimes find personally (and therefore creatively) inhibiting.

As Rachel Lambert, MacInnes' contact in London during the crisis, explains:

"There is a difficult balance to maintain between handholding when it is needed and peering over their shoulder when they are happier to be left to it – both of which are now far easier to do with e-mail. They do want someone to say yes to everything they do but it is often nice to have someone to bounce ideas off. Bruce wears his heart quite close to his sleeve and even if he does not always admit it himself, it is good to have someone behind him confirming that he is going in the right direction."

This leads us right into the heart of the second caveat about e-mail and the Internet as a creative medium. In practice, its potential is largely dictated by the way it is used and regulated by the organization.

In large organizations, most electronic communications are conducted through corporate intranets or discussional databases. New software developed in the millennium year has made it possible for senior management to screen incoming traffic. Although this has mainly been done to protect the legal position of the organization – for example, to prevent staff from downloading pornographic or pedophilic material – the unintended byproduct is often to shut down the uninhibited and free-wheeling use by staff of e-mail as a creative medium.

In one well-known US research institute with whom we collaborate, it is technically an offense for staff to receive – not just to send – e-mail messages that contain swear words. A senior research fellow who recently conducted a *bona fide* study into companies' HIV screening was unable to save his work using the file names "HIV" or "Aids" because both words were prohibited on the organizational intranet. The introduction of screening of this kind, the researcher told us, had transformed staff's perception of e-mail from a liberating creative force to an Orwellian threat to their privacy. Staff were no longer willing to conduct creative discussions over the intranet because they could not express themselves in the way they wished among trusted colleagues, for fear that flippant or profane comments might be picked up by the software. He says:

"The feeling now is about the same as if all our phones were being bugged . . . Swear words in our department are a sign of acceptance and trust. They fuel creative discussions. E-mail originally enabled us to transfer some of the dynamic of this informality and "near the edge" exchanges into electronic form. Now we have to conduct all electronic discussions as if a senior director is present."

CASE STUDY: BRITISH AIRWAYS

When British Airways decided to break with tradition and create their own purpose-built headquarters in the early 1990s, a strong incentive for so doing was to eliminate the "turf wars" that had bedeviled the years leading up to its privatization in 1987 and to use the layout and facilities of the new building to foster greater staff creativity.

The general manager who spearheaded the initiative, Gwilym Rees-Jones, calculated that the organization could benefit to the tune of £3.5mn a year through the increased productivity that would result. Part of the strategy was to design a building with communal facilities that would be used by all staff for meetings and discussions, thus encouraging cross-departmental contact on a routine basis. This aspect of the initiative is highlighted in Chapter 6. The other part was to revolutionize office work through a dedicated electronic communications system.

The project team member responsible for the technology was the IT architecture and innovation manager, Phil Matthews. Taking advantage of a greenfield site, Matthews aimed to construct a purpose-built communications infrastructure that would underpin the culture and operations of the initiative, not only at the time of the launch but for a further decade. Five thousand gigabytes (5000GB) of computer memory and 168km of copper cabling was calculated to provide computer support for at least double the number of expected occupants, to allow for rapid growth.

Among the more important systems developed by Matthews was a digitally enhanced cordless (DEC) phone system, combined with quest and communications points that allowed staff to conduct phone and video conversations from anywhere in the building; and a new electronic diary system that, at the time it was developed, prompted a revolution in personal planning at BA in what had until then been a desk and pocket diary culture.

The people dimension was handled by a trio of managers: facilities manager Alison Hartigan, organization behavior advisor Jan Dunn, and external architect and office design expert Kathy Tilney. Together they designed a scheme called "club working," based on what they had learned about hot-desking in companies around Europe including the

Danish hearing aid manufacturer Oticon and the Dutch insurance giant Interpolis.

Under the scheme, staff keep their essential possessions in a filing drawer and then pick the work area most suited to their immediate needs. The area closest to the entrance of all offices, at the center of the building, is designed for communal socializing, with drinks machines and coffee tables. The area in the middle of each office provides staff with the facilities they need for computer work, either through terminal points designed for "touchdown" contact such as checking or responding to messages or diary requests; or for desktop computer work using facilities that need to be booked, rather like a tennis or squash court booked at a sports club. The outer area, overlooking a 100ha (240acre) landscaped park open to the public, is designed for private study.

Club working was piloted with great success by the relationship marketing department in the run up to the launch of the building in July 1998. All of the 3,500 staff initially earmarked for relocation to Waterside were provided with training in how to use the new system to minimize paper and streamline communications.

However, it was not all plain sailing. The relationship marketing department, in retrospect, was the easy option when it came to piloting the scheme. Highly peripatetic, with much of their work conducted outside the office, they were bound to respond well to any system that enabled them to keep in touch at a distance. Other departments were cautious or even hostile. The idea of using communal social facilities received a big thumbs up from most of the staff (see Chapter 6), but members of work units that stayed physically in one place to do their work disliked the "club" principle. Both the finance and legal departments demanded, and got, a reversion to a one-person-one-desk approach.

The impact of electronic communications on the creative output of staff is still under review. However, BA are aware of other schemes which have produced, at best, ambiguous results – and this review is facing sudden and unexpected problems because the future of Waterside is now under question in the wake of the crisis provoked by the events of September 11 2001 (see Introduction).

However, even setting aside the impact of world events, BA was already aware of other virtual working schemes which have produced, at best, ambiguous results. The Scottish Development Agency, which attracts and allocates investment into developing regions in the country, recently piloted a very similar scheme to BA's. The evaluation, after two years, suggested that while communications between members of existing teams and work units improved greatly, creative interchanges between groups or individuals that did not already know each other were unaffected by the provision of new technology alone.

Individuals, argued organizer Ros Southgate, remain individuals. They will only use a new medium for creative interchange if they personally feel comfortable with it – yet another reason why, in the quest for the innovative individual, organizations need to focus on the word *individual* before they start getting carried away by the word *innovative*.

KEY LEARNING POINTS

» E-mail and intranet working opens up new possibilities for creative interchanges across different departments, sites, and countries.

» These exchanges are enriched because staff who are comfortable with the medium are able to capture what they are thinking as they are thinking it, unconstrained by the filtering and self-censuring earlier generations use when committing their thoughts to paper.

» Being able to "bond" over the Internet presupposes that the interchange is confined to individuals that the sender knows and trusts. Excessive regulation of e-mail traffic, using software designed to screen all incoming and outgoing messages to prevent illegal activity like the downloading of pornography, may unwittingly infringe on the private "space" needed for the interaction.

The Global Dimension of the Innovative Individual

» Globalism as a one-sided affair.
» Case study: fighting over the lighting industry in Hungary.
» From conformity to diversity.
» Diversity as a creative force.
» Case study: diversity and product development in a cosmetic company.

The impact of globalism on the innovative individual has in many ways reflected the move from top-down conformity to bottom-up discretion that was previously described in Chapter 3.

When the political events of the late 1980s opened up the emerging markets of Asia and Eastern Europe, large Western corporations operating in those areas had one overwhelming priority: to exert as much control and conformity as possible among local suppliers and staff who lacked training and an understanding of the international quality standards that the developed world had adopted in recent years.

A ONE-SIDED AFFAIR

It was a peculiarly one-sided affair. In key areas like manufacturing, hotels and tourism, catering, and entertainment, the products and services were those of North America and Europe, and the standards that dictated how staff were recruited and trained were those of the Western-based International Standards Organization (ISO). In support services like management consulting and financial services, the strategy adopted by leading players was based on the assumption that key clients had a global presence and would require a consistent, identical service from their suppliers regardless of the physical location of the office or practice with whom they were dealing.

Of course this required "gatekeepers": people who spoke the language, understood the locals, talked the language of the national or provincial government, were able to advise clients or internal managers about local markets, and who generally gave the aura of a multi-ethnic firm.

In the early 1990s, firms made do with exiles (for their forays into Eastern Europe) or, in the case of China, Hong Kong or Singaporean Chinese to fill the "gatekeeper" role. But when it became clear that these managers lacked the inside knowledge of their parent company's territory, or were regarded with outright hostility by the inhabitants, corporations started recruiting "true" locals and training them to their own standards.

In a survey on expatriate managers, conducted by the authors for the Economist Intelligence Unit (EIU) in 1994, 66% of the companies surveyed stated they were using more locally-recruited Asian and Chinese professionals in overseas assignments because they were trying to be more systematic in building pan-regional or international management teams.

In China, a cut-throat battle was fought in the mid-1990s for the limited number of PRC (mainland) graduates with an MBA education. A fledgling international business school, set up by the European Union in Shanghai, reported in 1997 that their graduates in employment were being offered three times their current salary to change jobs. In the same year, the EIU reported that turnover in foreign ventures in China was over 30% per year.

But the point to note is that these managers were acting as brokers, gatekeepers, and pulsetakers for products, services, and ways of working that had been developed by their employers in another world. The training and development they received, in common with all other employees of the corporation, was to conduct business the company way.

For most of the 1990s, globalism was about being seamless and consistent. Large corporate training centers located in the corporation's home territory – like Andersen Consulting's training center at St Charles in Illinois and General Electric's corporate "university" at Crotonville – existed to instill the philosophy of business developed by senior management or the founder, not to exchange new ideas and insights from the front line.

HUNGARIAN ORTHODOXY

"Think global, act local" was the mantra of the decade. However, what most firms failed to realize was that thinking global made it almost impossible to act in a way that took into account local needs or local ideas.

General Electric's takeover of the Hungarian lightbulb manufacturer Tungsram in 1991 is a good case in point. Originally acquiring a 50% share of the company in 1989, as part of an early push to build a base in the lighting industry outside the US, GE took over the company two years later when the Comecon economic system collapsed and with it Tungsram's Eastern European markets.

GE's operations throughout the world follow the simple formula of its illustrious chief executive, Jack Welch. If a business is not first or second in its market, close it, sell it, or fix it. Break down all internal barriers to action and communication. Become a "boundaryless" organization, shifting resources and expertise to wherever they are most needed.

Accordingly, the Tungsram turnaround followed a familiar pattern: divestment, integration, cost-cutting, plus large-scale investment in infrastructure, training, and research. A total of $600mn was invested in Tungsram's core factories. Assembly line workers and supervisors were trained in the latest Western approaches to quality management and teamwork.

However, as part of the disinvestment program, 50% of the workforce – almost 9,000 workers – was laid off. This was no more than was happening elsewhere in Hungary and other Central European countries. But the deal with General Electric, which involved a relaxation of the labor laws and tax breaks, had been sold to the workforce and the government as a means of saving jobs.

George Selmeczy, president of the Independent Tungsram Trade Union, stated in 1994:

> "When GE acquired a majority shareholding of Tungsram in 1989 it was hailed as a shining example of how capitalist prosperity could be brought to post-Communist central Europe. But at the time GE assumed full ownership of the company in 1993, much of the deal's luster had failed in the wake of the job cuts. Tungsram workers felt increasingly betrayed by American management."

The sense of the prevailing culture being American rather than global was not helped by phrases such as "empowerment" and "a culture of winning." To senior GE executives, these were articles of faith, involving a commitment to improvement that is continuous and not linked to specific wage deals. To Tungsram workers they bore a confusing similarity to slogans of the old order – which of course were bypassed or ignored – or another way of increasing responsibilities without any reward.

This would not have mattered in the long term had the commitment of GE's senior "American" managers and the junior and middle Hungarian managers been to the same goal. The attitude of Hungarian managers, staff and politicians was that the GE purchase of Tungsram was for the benefit of their own country. However, to Charles Pieper, the head of GE Lighting Europe, who was based 1450km (900m) away in London, it was part of a Europe-wide fight for market dominance against rivals Osram and Philips.

As part of this fight, drawing on Jack Welch's concept of "boundary-less," he saw newly trained Hungarian managers as the company's front line in their next wave of acquisitions in the newly created territories of Russia and the CIS republics. In an interview for the UK's leading business journal *Management Today* (conducted by the authors) he commented:

> "The Hungarian team will support the Russian operation in the way our US managers supported change at Tungsram – by transferring know-how."

But the point to note is that this know-how is not that of the Hungarian team. It is *American*. The team members were merely passing on the lessons they themselves had learned. Nothing was picked up on the way in terms of how business should work in the region. Welch's concept that staff should draw on and share good practice wherever they found it broke down in Hungary, because his senior managers did not perceive there was anything local worth knowing. As one of the Hungarian project managers, Tibor Fricsan, commented:

> "Our world totally changed. We gained greatly in terms of more training, a better work environment, and more generous pay. But there was the feeling that we had very little to offer in terms of our own knowledge or know-how. We were the pupils and the Americans were the teachers and this resulted in a passivity that did not always serve the company very well."

Passivity is hardly what a company wanting to share good practice and knowledge is after. As innovation moved higher up the corporate agenda in the late 1990s, organizations began to see the individuality of their managers and their workers as an asset, not a liability. In the process, the single most important attribute of a globally-recruited, multi-ethnic workforce moved from being the consistency of their performance to the diversity of their perspective.

DIVERSITY AS A CREATIVE POWERHOUSE

Diversity as a powerhouse of creative insight was hardly new. As far back as the late 1970s, the possibilities had been recognized by the well-known case of Tame Hair Cream Rinse, a hair conditioning product made by Gillette that at that time was a dying brand. Jackie Butler, a black female account executive at J. Walter Thompson, the company's advertising agency, persuaded Gillette to target its efforts at the Afro-American female market. The result was a significant extension of the product's life cycle without any change in the formulation or packaging.

However, this was seen as a highly focused solution to a highly focused problem: if you want to target a black female market, bring in a black female manager to do it because she will understand the market best.

What has changed since the late 1990s is that organizations have recognized that having a diversity of people on creative teams is, in itself, bound to lead to a broader range of solutions. It is also less likely to lead to the kind of corporate hindsight that executives like Intel's Andy Grove and commentators like Stanford University's Richard Pascale believe to have been the death of so many big-name companies with long track records.

Andy Grove has good reason to know this. Intel's Pentium chip was the brainchild of the company's first global product development team, and such teams are now an essential part of the company's product development effort.

In the same way, Standard Chartered Bank has launched a global in-company MBA, which is available to aspiring senior managers in locations as diverse as Tokyo, Kuala Lumpur, Nairobi, and London. Although much of the coursework is conducted virtually through the Internet, teams of these managers are brought together to conduct strategic assignments – and have learned from each other's good practice. The approach to individual customer service adopted by the bank's Asia – Pacific operation, which has a strong high-street presence, has helped to transform the corporate banking services provided by its European division.

TAPPING THE CULTURAL MIX

The case for tapping diversity across international boundaries has been supported all the more forcibly because the most creative regions in any country usually boast the highest ethnic mix. In London, a city with 50 different communities and where over 200 languages are spoken, multiculturalism is proving an important magnet for inward investment. The US software service company Syntel chose the British capital as the base for its European operations in 1997 precisely because of its cosmopolitan nature.

Similar reasons were given by Delta Airlines when it was choosing a location for a central telephone-reservations operation for Europe. "We selected London because we felt the large multilingual workforce was an important key to our success," says regional director Mary Smith. Previously, Delta had reservations offices in 12 European countries.

In the US, it is no coincidence that the creative force of the computer and telecommunications industries are in California and Texas, which have the highest concentration of new ethnic communities from Asia – Pacific. A recent survey by the top business journal *Fortune* estimated that 33% of all successful businesses in Silicon Valley were founded by first or second generation Americans from the Pacific Rim.

Michael Eisner, the man who turned Disney around in the 1980s and whose search for new ideas amounts to little short of a crusade, acknowledges the enormous importance of a diverse workforce to his own company. During a recent interview for *Harvard Business Review*, he said:

"I'm not just talking about diversity in skin color or ethnic background, I'm talking about diversity as a point of view. We want people who work here to look at the world differently from each other. They can be white, they can be Afro-American, they can be Indian or Chinese or Latino – it doesn't really matter. The important thing is that they look at the same problem and bring their own individuality to the solution."

CASE STUDY: L'ORÉAL

L'Oréal, the number one producer of beauty products since 1978, has founded its success on a steady stream of new products and a rapid expansion into Europe, the Americas, and Asia during the 1990s.

The company now boasts 400 subsidiaries, 500 brands, and representatives in 150 countries. It comprises four main cosmetics divisions:

Salon, Consumer, Perfumes, and Beauty and Active Cosmetics. L'Oréal also operates in pharmaceuticals, dermatology, and related fields, and it attaches a high priority to research activities leading to new product developments.

In these circumstances, the managers and the professionals it recruits are expected to have a solid knowledge of expert knowledge about the properties of the product for which they are responsible – and also the ability to tailor their sales approach to meet high localized needs.

Philippe Louvet, director of human resources for L'Oréal's consumer products division at the group's headquarters in Clichy, a decidedly unchic suburb of Paris, reports that:

> "All our managers must have a broad international and intercultural approach to their work. Our managerial staff already cover a very wide range of different European backgrounds. We are now looking for more people from Asia and the Americas, in particular to support our business expansion in these regions."

In pursuit of this goal, the company's head office reflects the greatest possible mix of nationalities and backgrounds. For example Louvet's own department includes the following: a 28-year-old woman with an Oxford University degree in French and Latin; an Italian who studied music and then took a business course at the French business school HEC; an executive with dual Japanese and US nationalities; plus Portuguese, Greek, and Vietnamese nationals.

L'Oréal's philosophy is that diversity is not about race, sex, language, or work background. It is about perspective and how this influences the way the organization thinks collectively. It maintains ongoing contact with a large and diverse number of higher education institutions from which it recruits its managers. These include fashion and design schools in Britain and France and technical and scientific institutions in Germany.

It offers graduates from these establishments no special help or career path and requires them to start from scratch as entry-level sales representatives. The company's director of human resources comments:

"Our current chief executive loves to remark that L'Oréal managers must be both 'poètes et paysans' (poets and men of the soil). It is the diverse way in which these people from different backgrounds and different countries react to a common set of experiences that keeps the flow of ideas alive."

KEY LEARNING POINTS

» Globalism in its early stages was founded on the need for cross-boundary consistency in quality and service provision. Now it is being enriched by a new quest for diversity in thought and perspective.

» Some of the best products in the international marketplace, such as Intel's Pentium Chip and L'Oréal's skincare products, have been created by global product development teams that benefit from the insight that comes from members with different backgrounds, traditions, and outlooks.

» The important thing is not simply the insight a multi-ethnic or multi-lingual team brings about in different taste and preferences. It is, to quote Disney's Michael Eisner, the capacity of each individual to "look at the same problem and bring their own individuality to the solution."

The State of the Art of Individual Innovation

» Eliminating a blame culture.
» Discouraging black and white thinking.
» Encouraging people to share information and ideas.
» Mandating managers to champion and foster creativity.

The prevailing thought about innovation and the individual, highlighted in Chapter 2, is that instead of focusing on identifying and developing a discrete group of "innovative individuals," organizations would do better to create a working environment in which all employees are able and willing to tap their own creative potential.

It follows that much of the state-of-the-art practice in the past five years has revolved around both eliminating those aspects of daily working that constrain or inhibit creative thinking, and introducing initiatives that foster it. The factors on which organizations or commentators have focused the most are summarized below.

ELIMINATING BLAME

A blame culture affects how people think and what they do. People will not experiment in their work in such a culture because it carries the risk of failure. They fear the embarrassment and loss of status it brings. Organizations often reinforce this natural tendency when they promote a commitment to "error free" work or announce a "zero tolerance for failure" ethic, as many did under Total Quality Management (TQM) initiatives in the 1980s.

Undoing the damage is often far harder than doing it in the first place. If managers want their staff to test out good ideas at work, they have to be very explicit in reassuring them that there will be no comeback if anything goes wrong. This was the overwhelming conclusion of a study recently carried out by Fiona Lee, an assistant professor of psychology at the University of Michigan in Ann Arbor, who, with two colleagues from Harvard Business School, looked at how hidden assumptions undermined a new initiative at a large US midwestern healthcare organization.

The organization had recently introduced a Web site that would provide medical staff and administrators with a single access point for retrieving the most up-to-date clinical information. Because there was no formal training course for the system, employees had to experiment with it to gain proficiency.

In a survey of 688 staff – covering 5 teaching hospitals, 30 health-care centers, and 120 outpatient clinics – Lee and her colleagues assessed how each person used the technology and how this use was influenced by the management culture in their work units. She found that individuals were more willing to experiment with the new system – trying out different software applications and testing new system features – when their departmental managers did two things: state explicitly that making mistakes would be okay, and refrain from punishing employees over errors.

Managers who gave mixed signals, such as verbally encouraging experimentation while keeping in place a reward system that punished failure, created mistrust and confusion. The effects of inconsistent messages was particularly strong among junior staff. Medical students, for example, assumed that failed experiments could harm their careers because of the need to demonstrate their competence in front of their peers in order to win advancement. By contrast, Lee found employees who were "allowed the room to fail" ended up being the most proficient and satisfied with the new technology – and the quickest to integrate it into their everyday work.

The financial cost of failure is another part of the equation. Most manufacturing companies keep a tight control on experimentation because of the research, prototyping, and training required to test and refine unproven ideas. The price tag can dampen down the willingness of R&D staff to try out wild ideas that, once in a while, will lead to a major breakthrough.

For example, at BMW's research and development center in Munich (see detailed case study in Chapter 7) one psychological barrier to off-the-wall experimentation with car components is that every proto-type requires a new set of tools or models, which are expensive to manufacture and will be scrapped if the experiment is abandoned. Using molded plastic that can be sculpted to a high standard of proficiency by laser design tools, BMW have found a way of reducing the costs of early experiments. Staff now feel freer to spend a couple of days exploring the manufacturing implications of a new component that emerges, for example, out of a creative brainstorm – because the only cost to the company is their time.

DISCOURAGING BLACK AND WHITE THINKING

Physicist turned management guru Danah Zohar (see detailed case study in Chapter 8) points out that most management thinking owes its origins to the Newtonian theories of science that dominated North American and European universities in the late nineteenth century.

This taught that all matter is simple, law-abiding, and ultimately controllable. But in a time of constant change, when innovation is at a premium, a more useful foundation for management thought is that of quantum physics, which teaches that all things are complex, chaotic, and uncertain.

Newtonian thinking suggests that there is one best way to get from A to B. Quantum thinking encourages people to think that there are many equally valid ways. Newtonian thinking stresses that any problem can best be solved by breaking it into smaller parts and examining each in turn. Quantum thinking encourages managers to look at the relationship between these parts.

Zohar argues that black and white thinking is still prevalent in professions like law, accountancy, and banking, where rationality and analysis forms the foundation for the way the profession is taught. Because these professions are still the most common recruiting ground for management positions, this view of the world remains deeply rooted in business.

Creative discussions are problem-solving exercises that are dominated by the idea that you do not volunteer any contribution that has not been thought through or supported by a rational argument. Yet proponents of lateral thinking, such as Alex Osborne in the 1960s or Edward de Bono in the 1970s and 1980s, stress that this form of censorship – by colleagues or the individual originating the thought – is guaranteed to discourage "out-of-the-box" thinking.

Osborne in particular stresses that it is not the quality of thoughts that matter but the volume. Wild, unworkable ideas act as a bridge to insights that are more practical. These insights will not be reached without the change in perspective that the wilder thoughts bring with them. The purpose of any creative discussion should be to encourage all participants to say, literally and with the license of others in the group, the first thing that comes into their minds.

This requires trust, confidence, and no fear of ridicule. In a truly creative exchange, Osborne argues, everyone should suspend judgment. Anything goes – there is no *wrong* idea. Once the idea is expressed, it should not be held onto by the individual who originated it. Participants should build on each other's ideas, abandoning any attempt to "own" or protect any idea that emerges.

It also requires the right management culture to underpin it. Few companies, for example, practice brainstorming more enthusiastically than IDEO, an industrial design company. Founded by David Kelly in 1978 and based in Palo Alto, IDEO has launched a stunningly diverse range of products, from the Polaroid I-Zone Camera to Crest Toothpaste's Neat Squeeze tube.

At IDEO, the rules of brainstorming are strictly observed. Design teams are expected to make mistakes early and often. Coming to the "right" solution too quickly is discouraged. Team members are encouraged to question any and all assumptions about what innovation means. At IDEO, people are not deemed to be innovative unless they are challenging the client's, the team's, and their own pre-existing notions.

Paradoxically this means that during brainstorms, any notions other than standard company or industry orthodoxies are given an open hearing. David Kelly argues that innovation is not just about surprising ideas, it is about surprising *people* – and that fostering innovation is mainly about encouraging people to relate to each other in creative ways. "Being a design genius is great," he concludes. "Being a design genius at the expense of the team is not."

ENCOURAGING PEOPLE TO SHARE

This, in turn, means that individuals have to be willing to share their insights. Morten Hansen, of Harvard Business School, recently combined forces with Bolko von Oetinger, a senior vice-president in the Munich office of the Boston Consulting Group, to promote the need for what they call "T-shaped managers."

These are people who share knowledge freely across the organization (the horizontal part of the "T") while remaining committed to the performance of their own business unit (the vertical part). As Hansen puts it, the successful T-shaped manager must learn to live with, and ultimately thrive within, the tension caused by this dual responsibility.

His theories are based on work with a number of international organizations who have identified the need for cross-boundary knowledge sharing, at a time when organizations are growing more delayered, international, and virtual. These include GlaxoSmithKline, who have recently encouraged the "cross-pollination" of ideas through information matchmakers working across different divisions and countries; Siemens, who have launched a training program that brings high-potential managers from different divisions in small teams to solve specific problems raised by individual business units; and global steel-makers Ispat, whose board has introduced cross-directorships, requiring the general manager of every operating unit to sit on the board of at least one other unit.

However, the decision to share insights and knowledge is not simply a matter of managers responding to a new corporate initiative. It is a matter of individual choice. Researchers at the Roffey Park Institute in the UK have identified two ways in which individuals' willingness to contribute their creativity to their organization is cut short.

The first is "psychological withdrawal," where uncertainty about their personal future in the organization due to change of any kind leads to fear and stress and, as a consequence, inhibition in the work. The second is "psychological work to rule," where more confident staff deliberately hold back their best ideas until they can ascertain what personal benefits the change will bring – using their creative insights to start up their own enterprise or to win themselves a better position in a competitor firm should the outcome not suit their needs.

Either way, the innovative capability of the individual is lost to the firm. Wendy Hirsh and Marion Devine from the Roffey team argue that this is one reason why so many mergers fail. The uncertainty surrounding the talks, often communicated to staff only through company gossip or press reports, undermines the very capability that the union is designed to exploit. Hirsh and Devine stress that this phenomenon will only be countered if the companies take the time and effort to reassure staff about their future *at the start of the process* and not, as is so often the case, only once the deal is completed. This also counts in the case of any other initiative that, in the eyes of the individual, will affect his or her future career.

In exactly the same way, the process of job cutbacks and promotion freezes that followed in the wake of the economic slowdown in the latter half of 2001 has either been hindered or eased by the level of transparency with which they have been implemented. UCLA

Professor Karen Stephenson's work on the value of "gatekeepers" and "pulsetakers" in organizational networks (see Chapter 8) was inspired during the recession of the early 1990s when these key individuals, whose cross-functional positions enable them to communicate with staff across the whole organization, were used to counter the rumor mill and prevent in the process a hemorrhaging of creative talent.

REWARDING AND RECOGNIZING CREATIVE CONTRIBUTIONS

The flip side of the coin is making individuals feel it is worth their while making the creative effort. This can be achieved in a variety of different ways.

The first, common to manufacturing companies, is through ideas competitions or reward schemes. Nucor, once a small player in the US steel industry, has helped transform both itself and the whole industry through the systematic encouragement of innovation in the front line.

A young engineer working at the Arkansas plant at Blytheville recently saved the company more than $1mn by inventing tapered pieces of metal called shims, which require no lubrication and are therefore cheaper to maintain than the screws used to support steel mill machinery that were designed for the plant by the manufacturers. More importantly, a team of engineers working at the Crawfordsville plant in Indiana developed a technique called thin-slab casting, which enabled Nucor to compete effectively in flat-rolled steel manufacturing at a fraction of the cost experienced by bigger players.

In both cases, the breakthroughs were encouraged by an incentive scheme that pays workers up to twice their basic salary for any initiative that boosts the company's productivity. (For a more detailed case study of Nucor, see Chapter 7.)

Other manufacturers report similar breakthroughs. At the Norwegian shipbuilder Kvaerner, welder Arne Svennson was awarded a prize equivalent to US$3,800 in 1991 for an idea on how to automate the welding of a key component, which resulted in Kvaerner's subsidiary Kamfab saving US$45,000 a year. Two adjustable rotating welding tables invented by a pair of section managers in another shipbuilding subsidiary, conceived in 1994, have already saved the company nearly $5mn.

Harald Faru, Kvaerner's vice president of Intellectual Property, explains how these ideas came to light:

"The purpose of all our initiatives is to reach people who would not normally think of putting ideas in a suggestions box, and who come up with a stream of ideas in the course of their day-to-day work. While the prize money is always welcome, it is the opportunity to gain public recognition for the originality in the thinking that is the real incentive to take part."

As part of a modernization project, the Royal National Orthopaedic Hospital in the UK launched a major consultation exercise among its staff, backed by a suggestions scheme called "Say So" (i.e., if you think so, say so). They received valuable feedback on issues as varied as the likely effects on surgical operations of smart technology like tele-linkages to other sites and voice activation, and the way outpatient care will be transformed by telemedicine backed by peripatetic clinical support schemes.

This feedback has informed and inspired new multi-disciplinary teams that worked with other hospitals to examine the practical implications. Phyllis Shelton, director of business development, says of the Say So project:

"This is an exciting project involving all staff to look critically at what they do and take greater control ... It is inspiring what can be done simply by sharing good ideas and by approaching change in bite-size pieces."

Harald Faru's comment, that it is the recognition that counts as much as the reward, is reflected in computer company Nortel Networks' "Intellectual Property Awards and Recognition" plan, designed to recognize and reward individuals working for the company who have successfully had patent applications granted.

In addition to being given a sizeable cash bonus, sometimes in excess of £10,000, the inventor receives a plaque which celebrates the patent and is presented by senior executives at a special ceremony attended by other patent awardees. This is often held at a location of scientific or engineering significance. In the UK, for example, ceremonies have recently taken place at Greenwich Observatory, the Thames Barrier, and Bletchley Park, where the German code Enigma was cracked during World War II.

A further way of rewarding inventive staff, given MIT research that suggests creative people want to follow their own leads, is to support work in which they have a personal stake. Hewlett-Packard allows, and often funds, its top scientific staff to travel and take sabbaticals, and even nominates the academic collaborators with whom they would like to work. Going further along the same lines, there is also widespread encouragement to publish scientific papers, take part in international conferences and seminars, and play leading roles in the formulation of industry standards.

MANDATING MANAGERS TO FOSTER IDEAS

None of these initiatives would work if managers and supervisors did not take a lead both in encouraging individuals to push out their creative boundaries and in championing the results.

Our own research (see Chapter 8) suggests that this is seen as a discretionary activity, to be indulged in when managers have the time or inclination, rather than an essential role. As the chairman of the British banking group Lloyds TSB Brian Pitman commented in 1999:

> "You have to make sure that whatever idea is put forward, you give it a response – every time. If people put a suggestion forward and they don't get a response – even if it's negative and you explain why you are not going to do what is suggested – they'll think it is a waste of time trying."

Managers can foster the creativity of their staff in any number of ways.

» They can act as "sponsors," promoting the idea inside the organization, ensuring that it is not dismissed and sustaining interest during prolonged periods of gestation.
» They can act as "sounding boards," allowing the person with the idea to draw on their broader knowledge or impartial viewpoint to inform or validate the premise or to comment on the practicalities.

» As a member of a project development team or on a one-to-one basis, they can help "shape" the idea, fleshing out the premise or finding practical ways to make it "real."
» They can bring their specialist knowledge to bear – for example in technology, law, or finance – to underpin its implementation or provide a particular perspective.

The transformation of working practices at British Airways through the imaginative design of its new Waterside headquarters (see case study in Chapter 4) was the brainchild of its property general manager, Gwilym Rees-Jones. He recognized that a routine relocation to avoid overcrowding could be turned into a heaven-sent opportunity to break down barriers and improve creativity if the building was purpose built for the task. Accordingly, he won the board's permission to design and construct the headquarters from scratch, using a layout that would ensure staff from different departments shared the same social facilities and used them for routine meetings.

In all, it took five years for Rees-Jones to get the green light and a further five for the building to be constructed. During the critical early years, when the proposal could easily have been dismissed as an expensive pipedream – the ultimate price tag was £200mn – Rees-Jones received support from a number of key people, both inside and outside the company.

The first step was to find vacant land on which to build the headquarters. The then chief executive Colin Marshall insisted that the new building must be adjacent to or within the Heathrow airport perimeter. All that was available was a derelict site at the far north-western end of Heathrow which, although it had been used as a rubbish tip by the construction company that owned it, was still designated a greenfield site by the local council.

Local residents were very suspicious of any further encroachment on their privacy by BA and raised strong objections to the sale of the site for commercial purposes. Most of the board, including the prospective successor to Colin Marshall, Bob Ayling, wrote off any prospect of Rees-Jones gaining planning permission. The proposal would have been dismissed there and then had not Rees-Jones received the unexpected support of the company finance officer, Gordon Dunlop, who argued that the land was being sold at a knock-down price and was a good investment in its own right. Dunlop continued to sponsor the proposal for the following two years, ensuring that it was aired at regular intervals.

The next step was to come up with a design that would meet Rees-Jones's objectives. In this, he was helped by two sources of expertise. In thinking through the relationship between working environment and creative interactions, he drew on the work of Dr Tadeusz Grajewski and Professor Bill Hillier of the UK's Bartlett School of Architecture. Their report *The Social Potential of Buildings* provided Rees-Jones with the knowledge he needed to draw up the right architectural proposal and they acted as advisors and commentators when he created a business plan to put before the board.

Rees-Jones's proposals were theory at this stage. He needed an architect who could make it real. He found the right person in Niels Torp, a little-known Norwegian who had designed the SAS headquarters and whose background in town planning made him sensitive to the role of human behavior in shaping building designs.

Torp's designs envisaged six self-contained business units connected to each other by "The Street," a 175m long tree-lined boulevard with its own newsagent, bank, travel office, florist, supermarket, restaurant, and health and beauty salon. Floors on different levels are connected by walkways studded with sofas, easy chairs, and coffee tables, providing easily-accessible stop-off points for casual encounters.

The flow of staff from different parts of the building is carefully channeled to ensure the communal areas are used to the maximum impact. It is not possible, for example, for people to travel directly by lift from the underground car park. They have to walk via The Street. Torp also designed a 100ha (240acre) park with lakes and waterways to surround the building. This is open to the public and went a long way towards winning BA the planning permission it needed to proceed with the project.

Rees-Jones now had the site, the architectural designs, and planning permission. All that was left was winning the board's permission to go ahead. The financial plan he proposed to lay before the directors was based on the initial investment of £200mn being offset by measurable savings of £11.5mn a year through the closure of other leased sites and the money BA would save by not having to upgrade them on a routine basis. He also argued that an estimated £3.5mn a year would be saved through an annual 2% rise in productivity brought about by better creativity and motivation.

It was a difficult case to make as the most controversial element – the £3.5mn annual saving – was based on a hypothesis that could not be demonstrated on paper. In preparing his argument, Rees-Jones was greatly helped by a dress rehearsal in front of the retiring chairman Lord King, who was a confirmed sceptic. Rees-Jones won him around and the resulting boost to his confidence and the opportunity to refine his presentation went a long way towards securing the board's permission.

The five-year campaign by Rees-Jones to put Waterside on the map – it has lived up to his expectations although its future is currently under question (see Introduction) – shows that it is not enough for a single person, however creative, to come up with an idea that will make a difference. He or she needs the support of a variety of individuals who may have to stick their necks out to make the concept a going concern. If managers do not see this encouragement as part of their role, the opportunity for their organizations to fully exploit the creativity of their workforce becomes a lottery – dependent on having the right person in the right place at the right time.

KEY LEARNING POINTS

» Individuals will not feel enabled to take risks if they think they will be blamed if something goes wrong. They will judge whether this is the case not by what managers say but by what they do. Calls for greater creativity need to be matched by policies and actions that recognize and celebrate successes and enable both staff and management to learn from failures.

» Black and white thinking, particularly the kind that prejudges "out-of-the-box" hypothesis, is the enemy of creativity. Creative exchanges should be predicated on the principle that there is no such thing as a "bad" idea and that off the wall thoughts, however impractical, act as a bridge to new insights and perspectives that may lead to valuable breakthroughs.

» Rewarding individuals for their creative contributions is important because it demonstrates that the organization recognizes that these contributions are discretionary and given because the individual feels motivated and intellectually engaged by their work. An "award" is as important as "reward" because it makes the individual feel valued rather than simply being paid to be creative.

» Line managers can stifle the creativity of their staff at birth, whatever the overall philosophy of the organization. They should be mandated to foster and support innovation in their work units - by championing, advising, and shaping the ideas of their staff - rather than seeing this as a purely discretionary role.

Success Stories of Individual Innovation

» Lufthansa: using trust as a structure in a global alliance.
» BMW: creating serendipity in R&D.
» Nucor Steel: rewarding initiative on the front line.
» Shiseido: what motivates the innovative individual inside the organization.
» IntegriSys: what motivates the innovative individual outside the organization.

There follow five case studies to demonstrate the value of innovative individuals in practice.

LUFTHANSA: USING TRUST AS A STRUCTURE IN A GLOBAL ALLIANCE

"In a virtual business world, trust has become the surrogate for structure."

So says Thomas Sattelberger, human resources director at Lufthansa. It is a mantra he has used to help pilot Germany's national airline through a headlong rush towards the twenty-first century that has taken in cost-cutting, outsourcing, and a leading role in the world's largest airline alliance.

The strategic alliances that have revolutionized the airline industry are a logical byproduct of privatization. Until the late 1990s, despite some notable exceptions like British Airways and Scandinavian Airline Systems (SAS), the majority of European and Asian airlines were still state-controlled if not state-owned, and Byzantine regulations protected their home base while restricting their freedom of maneuver. But however slow and laborious the negotiations, controls are now being reduced and the airlines are becoming increasingly worried about their ability to compete and survive.

European airlines, facing high labor costs and overheads, were particularly vulnerable. By the mid-1990s, the cost of transporting an individual rose faster than the fares that passengers were prepared to pay. In 1997, Frank Reid, Lufthansa's president and chief executive commented:

"We are being hammered by the same market forces that are putting pressure on the whole industry. Airport charges, already too high, are rising by a further 24%. Space is at a premium and despite strenuous efforts on our part, we are only receiving 75% of the revenue from each ticket we sell."

In the circumstances, Reid was more than happy to take a leading role in setting up the Star Alliance in 1995, consisting of his own company and United Airlines, Scandinavian Airlines (SAS), Varig (of Brazil), Air

Canada, and Thai. Star is easily the largest alliance in terms of the number of companies involved. Unusually, there is no central authority. In terms of "soft" issues like customer service and relationship marketing, the strength of the network depends on its weakest link. There is no obvious mechanism for the stronger members like Lufthansa to exert pressure on the weaker airlines. Any improvement has to be achieved through sharing experience and best practice.

It is in this context that Sattelberger sees bottom-up innovation as an important asset for the Alliance. Lufthansa has encouraged initiative among front-line staff in its in-flight services for well over a decade. In addition it gained valuable experience in "borderless learning" in the early 1990s, when the company outsourced support functions such as check-in services, aircraft maintenance, and food service.

Surveys indicate that these services account for up to 66% of customers' stated flight satisfaction. So managers at Lufthansa have to provide what Sattelberger calls "network glue": designing seamless transnational structures to develop a global outlook in all staff and inspire the right level of customer service from the "absent ones" (staff not employed by Lufthansa but who perform important tasks on the company's behalf).

Drawing on this experience, Sattelberger designed a series of programs and events designed not only to instill an "Alliance mentality" among staff from different members of the Star conglomerate, but to encourage them to share their knowledge and experience. These included international roadshows to communicate the ideas and vision of the Alliance, cross-cultural workshops, and joint management development programs designed specifically to encourage executives from all member companies to work together in developing new strategies for the Alliance.

Sattelberger feels strongly that individuals only contribute their own insights and experience when they identify with the aims of the enterprise. He uses the word "feel" time and again, particularly when describing the task of creating a common identity among employees from different member companies:

"I can look at myself in many ways. I feel Bavarian because I am a citizen of Bavaria. I feel German because I have German nationality.

I feel European because my country is part of the European Union. In the same way, managers and employees in the new initiative are asking themselves whether they are part of Lufthansa Cargo, the Lufthansa Group or the Star Alliance. The key question for us is how we can create a common sense of identity and purpose and therefore a willingness to share their expertise – among flight attendants in Chicago, purchasing agents in India and maintenance staff in Beijing, this ensures common standards of reliability and quality across the whole network.''

BMW: CREATING SERENDIPITY IN R&D

The use of workspace design to promote a free flow of ideas and information between individuals in different functions profoundly influenced BMW, Germany's leading luxury car manufacturer, when it invested over DM1bn in a new R&D facility close to the company's corporate headquarters in Munich at the start of the 1990s.

The new center, built on a 26ha (64acre) greenfield site acquired from the US Air Force, was the major plank in BMW's strategy to reduce the time it takes to produce new ranges of car from scratch. Until the center was launched in 1990, BMW's research staff were located in 12 different sites around Munich and the poor communication this generated was seen as a strategic albatross around BMW's neck.

Dr Wolfgang Reitzle, the creator of the new center, called FIZ (Forschung Ingenieur Zentrum) was influenced by a piece of research undertaken by Boston's Massachusetts Institute of Technology in the late 1980s which suggested that 80% of ideas that led to breakthrough products or services were triggered by routine or chance encounters, for example, over a cup of coffee. He said at the time of the plant's launch in 1991 that:

''The effective flow of materials has long been understood as the governing factor in design manufacturing. In like manner, we have adopted the free flow of ideas as our design criterion''

Accordingly, three governing principles lay behind the creation of FIZ:

» Streamlining traditional hierarchies: BMW's strategy called for all the functions contributing to the development of new models, and those that supply them, to be brought physically together. These comprise research, development, technical planning, production engineering, quality assurance, value analysis and cost control, purchasing, logistics, patents, and personnel. The layout of the entire complex and the occupation of each building is governed by the sequence followed in the design and development of new cars and not, as in the past, considerations of organization hierarchy.

» Imaginative allocation of space: A detailed analysis was carried out of how new models are developed, to discover which members of staff communicated with each other most frequently. As a result, development design departments are now located adjacent to the corresponding production planning departments. The engineer responsible for car doors, for example, works next to the technical planner who will translate his or her work into a prototype model.

All design offices are housed on the same floor as their model workshop, to ensure that staff from each communicate with each other by the shortest possible route. This means, for example, that a designer with an idea for a novel type of engine bulkhead can stop for a minute or two, wander down the corridor and find out directly from the robotics researchers whether a robot capable of the contortions needed to install such a design is available or capable of being developed. In this way, design engineers are able to follow the entire process of a vehicle's construction more closely, from design model to pilot series, and to study the results of the designs at first hand whenever they choose.

» Appropriate building design: The layout of the buildings is designed to support this kind of cross-functional working. The site consists of a central workshop linked by covered walkways to a series of satellite five-storey offices. Imaginative use of open-plan working areas, with few permanent structural walls, means that project teams can be created precisely according to requirements, without the need for structural modifications or the upheaval, dirt, and noise caused by building work.

The complex also incorporates a fully-fitted car assembly line capable of producing more than 3000 cars a year. As Hans Honig, manager of welding and joining systems, explains:

"This acts as a live 'testing ground,' enabling designers to check how and in what conditions the parts they have designed are fitted on the assembly line, hand-in-hand with members of staff who are being trained to oversee the production of the new series. Because production methods and procedures are tested in realistic conditions, problems can be identified and dealt with at an early stage, so that the start of production in other plants is much smoother."

A decade on, the plant has more than justified the time and financial resources BMW invested in building it. The highly popular "3-series" model was designed and developed at FIZ, as was the covered motor-bike featured in the James Bond film *Tomorrow Never Dies*. An innovative gas-charged lighting system and new welding and joining techniques are now being used on all models. Thanks to the methods pioneered at FIZ, the company is also already making recyclable cars, and designers at the center are now concentrating on making BMW cars both "greener" and safer.

Most importantly the development time taken by BMW to create new models – determined largely by the right innovative individual speaking to the right innovative counterpart in the right environment at the right time – has been reduced by 50%. Dr Bernd Pischetsrieder, the company's chairman and former director of manufacturing, argued in 1998 that the design and manufacturing methods used at FIZ would reduce by a full two years the development time of a new series to full production – giving the company a critical competitive edge in a country where labor costs are higher than anywhere else in the world.

NUCOR STEEL: REWARDING INITIATIVE ON THE ASSEMBLY LINE

When Ken Iverson, Nucor's longest serving chief executive, was awarded the US National Medal of Technology – the first steelman to be honored in this way – he accepted the award from President George Bush (senior) on behalf of the whole Nucor workforce.

Nucor has no R&D department or corporate engineering group. On average, 99% of the research and development work is done by the line. As he received the award from President Bush, Iverson commented:

"While the real technological breakthroughs have been the result of lengthy and sometimes frustrating initiatives involving senior executives and various specialists from inside and outside the company, there is also the recognition that everyday insights can lead to important innovations."

A good example is the invention of "shims." A young engineer at the company's Arkansas plant at Blytheville was part of a team taking part in a joint venture with Yamata Kogyo of Japan to produce beams, pilings, and heavy structural products. Aware that Nucor was spending $1.5mn a year on lubricating and maintaining supporting screws under part of the steel manufacturing equipment, he pointed out that tapered pieces of metal, which he called shims, require no lubrication and work more effectively than the screws designed for the plant by the manufacturer. The resultant savings in downtime and maintenance costs were worth more than $1mn.

Another example is "thin-slab casting," developed by a team of assembly line engineers at Nucor's plant in Crawfordsville, Indiana. This technique, long considered an impossible dream by other more traditional US mills, was considered so important to the long-term future of the steel industry that the US Government was about to carry out a study into its feasibility when Nucor first introduced it in the late 1980s. It involves casting steel in thin slabs, thus bypassing some of the most expensive machinery in a steel mill. At the time, steel was normally cast in thick slabs and then rolled until it was thin – with all the labor and costs entailed.

The attraction of the new process for Nucor was that it cut manufacturing costs by $50–$75 per ton. This enabled the company to get into the largest product area in the steel industry – flat rolled steel, which is extensively used in car bodies, steel cans, refrigerators and other white goods, and decks for building – and mount a serious challenge to big producers.

The initiative that led to the breakthrough was taken entirely by the engineers at one plant. Rex Querely, controller of the company's newest plant at Berkeley South Carolina, explains:

"If you want to try something new, if you want to try something innovative, it is done entirely on the mill floor. Crawfordsville got into thin-slab casting this way. The whole industry was talking about doing it. They just decided to try."

Despite the fact that it now has a turnover exceeding $50 bn, and is spread across several locations in the southern part of the US, Nucor has an old fashioned close-knit insular culture. It only has 7,000 employees and a headquarters staff of 22 at Charlottesville, North Carolina.

Iverson has worked hard to push responsibility down to the lowest possible level and uses strong incentives to focus everyone on productivity and earnings. Nucor workers have a low base salary of about 75% of the average for their industry, but the weekly bonuses related to productivity and efficiency mean they commonly make twice as much again – giving those at the South Carolina plant, for example, salaries in the past year of about $60,000.

Not surprisingly, this approach to incentive pay does not lend itself to collective bargaining and Nucor is avowedly anti-union.

SHISEIDO: WHAT MOTIVATES THE INNOVATIVE INDIVIDUAL INSIDE THE ORGANIZATION

In 1995, Japan's leading cosmetics manufacturer Shiseido launched a highly successful skin lotion called "Hadasui" (translates as "bare skin"). The campaign was notable for the fact that, for the first time in its history, the company based the launch around the originator, a 31-year-old marketing executive called Norika Shimada.

This was a significant break with the faceless traditions of the company, which reflected the mores of Japanese industry as a whole. In the previous two years the company had launched a series of successful products but at no point had they provided any public recognition for the originator.

The role Shimada played in the launch is a testament to the internal struggle she underwent to get the product approved by the board. "Hadasui"'s main ingredient is mineral water from the slopes of Mount Fuji. At the time, there was a boom in sales of mineral water in Japan and Shimada came up with the idea for the product after using mineral water in a number of ways at home.

The marketing concept behind "Hadasui" – that skin should have mineral water to "drink" too – did not go down well with Shiseido's conservative senior management. They felt that the message was too "faddy" and did not fit in well with the company's recent product launches.

Shimada had to lobby individual members of the board intensely with little or no help from colleagues in her own department. At the same time, she had to leave herself enough time to undertake her day-to-day work. In all, it took nearly a year of lobbying to get the product accepted and a further two years to get it on the market.

Shimada decided to use her own story as the centerpiece for the launch. This too was a departure from tradition. In the event, Japanese newspapers and magazines scrambled to get the story, resulting in major publicity and record sales for the product. Looking back, she says that:

> "The launch vindicated my persistence but it was a gamble. If you stick your neck out you have to risk it might get cut off."

Directors at Shiseido learned many lessons from the "Hadasui" launch, the most important being that individual recognition is vital in encouraging front-line staff to be more creative. In recent years, they have abolished the internal *sempai-kohai* relationships, where senior managers take precedence in all things, and are addressed by their rank by junior staff.

They have also learned from Shimada's experience that good ideas are often inspired outside the workplace and by making connections with ideas and experiences that are often unrelated to the company's sector or industry. To broaden their experience, senior managers at Shiseido now attend seminars where speakers discuss topics as diverse as international gymnastics and the work of Japan's volunteer medical service in developing countries.

INTEGRISYS: WHAT MOTIVATES THE INNOVATIVE INDIVIDUAL OUTSIDE THE ORGANIZATION

Creativity in most organizations results from the interplay between how an individual sees his or her work and the world that surrounds it and the organization's business priorities. As we saw in Chapter 6, most innovative decisions occur while the individual struggles to reconcile conflicting priorities, with the solution resulting from an unusual or unthought-of trade-off between these priorities.

The one constant is that the business priorities that trigger the process are those of the organization, not the individual. For example, taking some of the cases highlighted in this Chapter, the creation of BMW's research center by Dr Wolfgang Reitzle was prompted by the need for the company to reduce R&D time from inception to full production; the inspiration behind Shiseido's new Hadasui face lotion was generated by the company's need to gain a market lead in their Asia – Pacific markets; and the design of cross-company programs and roadshows at the Star Alliance by Thomas Sattelberger of Lufthansa was a logical response to the need for members of the alliance to share their experience and good practice.

In none of these cases did the individuals themselves create the priority or imperative. It was their job – by someone else's mandate – to find a solution, and the payback was promotion or a pay rise – again by someone else's mandate – together with a sense of internal satisfaction or professional pride.

In the case of entrepreneurs, the trigger for their creativity is very different. The priorities they struggle with are of their own making. The payback, while it may seem superficially similar – money, status, personal fulfillment – is different because it is not granted by someone else's mandate but won against the odds.

Marsha Sinetar of the Massachusetts Institute of Technology (see Chapter 8) identified three freedoms aspired to by all creative people: freedom in the way work gets done, freedom to ask novel and disturbing questions, and freedom to come up with unusual solutions to the things they're thinking about. These aspirations are also what turns them into entrepreneurs.

In most large organizations, these freedoms will be hedged in by caveats and qualifications. Someone else creates the rules. Even if this is not the case, someone else will have created the goals. That said, while the desire to set up their own enterprise may come early in an entrepreneur's life, it may take years or even decades to plan for. During this time, he or she will be refining the idea and gaining the necessary expert knowledge or financial resources. This might involve studying for an MBA, working for a variety of organizations, and building up the right professional network. Even young dotcom entrepreneurs are subject to a similar process. It is often the experience of building an independent life at college – involving a variety of semi-entrepreneurial activities like running a college band or organizing events – that triggers the desire to set up an enterprise, whether straight after college or a decade later.

This was certainly the case with Angus Friday, who first developed the desire to set up on his own while at medical school in his native Grenada. Aged 21, he set up Limelight Promotions, an events organization that soon stretched well beyond running college parties – so much so that Friday was contacted by the government of Grenada to develop, promote, and manage the island's Carnival City Festival in August 1987. A special cultural promotional event organized by the company the following year also won high praise in the local press.

Revenues from Limelight served the useful purpose of financing Friday's medical school living expenses. But it did not divert Friday from his mainstream career. There was never any doubt in his mind that healthcare would be the focus for his business acumen. The experience he picked up after he qualified only added to this certainty. Praised for his emergency management skills as a junior doctor at Grenada's General Hospital, he was voted onto the hospital management committee and later onto the board of the Grenada Medical Association.

The choice of the specific marketplace in this industry was inspired by what Friday learned on the strategy module of the MBA program at Strathclyde Business School, which Friday signed up for soon after he moved to the UK. He studied for the MBA with the specific intention of acquiring the necessary skills to set up a business of his own, at a time when the majority of MBA students saw the qualification as a passport to well paid salaried work in consultancies or investment banks.

As such, he did not benefit – as many MBA students do – from the experience and perspective of other participants. He focused entirely on what was taught by the tutors. He was most impressed by the strategy module, which was based in part on the "five forces" model of market behavior developed by Harvard's Professor Michael Porter. This postulated that if buyers aggregate their spending power in any industry, it creates opportunities for new sellers who can penetrate the market far faster than if spending power among buyers is dispersed.

Encouraged by his tutor, Professor Kees van der Heijden, Friday explored how this model might apply to the healthcare industry in the UK, where he intended to pursue his career. He devoted his project to researching a case study of how the Scottish Development Agency had used the aggregation of pharmaceutical research into cross-company collaborative projects to attract internal investment to the West of Scotland.

This provided him with a conceptual model for his own business. At this time in the UK, the practices of general doctors (GPs) had begun to group themselves into primary care groups that gave them greater buying power. Following the five-forces model of Porter, he realized that this provided new openings for anyone with services useful to GPs.

To explore these in greater depth, Friday took a job in the marketing department of a large UK-based pharmaceutical company, Merck Sharpe and Dohme. Here he helped to develop and launch a sales program aimed at the nascent primary care groups. The experience provided him with a better understanding of how the groups managed their spending budgets, plus a personal network that was to prove invaluable during the later development and piloting of the product that was to form the basis of his enterprise.

The idea for the product itself also came from the discussions with GPs from the care groups. It became very clear from their remarks that the ongoing professional development of doctors was as important as their initial medical education. The self-help revolution of the 1980s meant that patients were as informed as their GP, if not more so, about the latest developments in medical treatment. Rapid advances in pharmaceutical research were also making it hard for hard-pressed GPs to keep up.

Friday's concept was that his information could be provided on a Web-based service. No single trigger sparked the idea. However he did experience a breakthrough when he ordered by post Bill Gates' biography *The Road Ahead*,[1] complete with a CD-ROM in which Gates talked through the key points in the book.

It was the publisher's application of CD-ROM technology, rather than Gates' pearls of wisdom, that fired Friday's imagination. "It demonstrated what this technology was capable of," he says. "I have never forgotten it."

Friday set up his business in 1998 with the a grant of £100,000 from the UK's Department of Trade and Industry. Two years later he was able to expand the service using a further £750,000 of venture capital. He is currently looking to expand the business to Australia and New Zealand. At the time of writing, the company, IntegriSys, was valued at £7.5mn.

The decision to go "live" was a long time coming, as is often the case. But for the better part of a decade Friday planned for it. His decision to take an MBA and his decision to work for Merck Sharpe and Dohme were made with the sole purpose of giving him the skills, networks, and sector knowledge to launch his own enterprise. As he says himself:

"I never took my eye off the goal, and the goal was created in my own mind 20 years ago."

KEY LEARNING POINTS

» Opportunities for serendipitous encounters between staff from different companies should be built into the HR strategy underpinning any merger, acquisition, or alliance. This is particularly important for the exchange of best practice and insights into new markets (Lufthansa).

» Easy access to the individual with whom you want to exchange thoughts is a critical prerequisite. Buildings and workspace should be designed to eliminate features that will constrain or bar this access. These include long walks, corridors, closed doors, deep stairwells, and rapid changes in temperature (BMW).

» Schemes that reward and recognize initiatives and ideas are important if the organization wants to encourage innovation from the front line. Research and development staff will see the process of experimentation as a reward in its own right but staff who engage in less knowledge-intensive work will need more of an incentive (Nucor Steel).

» Involving the individual in the PR or marketing of the product or service that results is another boost to creativity. The encouragement of line managers to foster and support the ideas of their subordinates is all the more important in organizations where management traditions have been shaped by a hierarchical culture or background (Shiseido).

» Staff with entrepreneurial ideals or ambitions have their own agenda. The organization may wish to tap their creativity but they will also want to profit from the insight that working for the firm will give them into markets, methods, and networks. In the spirit of "employability" (see Chapter 8), this exchange of "favors" should be encouraged (IntegriSys).

NOTES

1 Gates, W. with Myhrvold, N & Rinearson, P. (1995) *The Road Ahead*. Full edn with CD-ROM. Viking, New York.

Key Concepts and Thinkers on the Innovative Individual

- » Emotional intelligence.
- » Empowerment.
- » How ideas are inspired.
- » Leadership and the innovative individual.
- » Networks and networking.
- » Spiritual intelligence.

Since the early 1990s, what we know about how individuals work innovatively in organizations has been transformed by a series of new concepts that owe very little to business school theory and more to a perspective of the organization by academic thinkers from the social or physical sciences.

Harvard University in particular has nurtured a number of scientists or philosophers turned business theorists whose view of individuals in organizations is based more on what is going on in their head, and the link this has to neuroscience, anthropology, and physics, than on the marketing, finance, or production imperatives to which they are subjected.

Groundbreaking research into how interactions occur between the parts of the brain responsible for rational thought and emotional response has shed new light on topics that were previously dismissed as incapable of useful analysis, such as insight, instinct, empathy, and holistic thinking. Here are a few of the concepts that have emerged.

EMOTIONAL INTELLIGENCE

This is probably the most influential concept to emerge on the innovative individual. The key thinker here is the US psychologist and former Wall Street journalist **Daniel Goleman** who, in the mid-1990s, looked at the personal profiles of top performers in 500 companies worldwide and found that a high IQ got the best managers only on the first rung of their chosen careers.

After that, personal qualities such as an ability to empathize with others and a grasp of the big picture counted for more than analytical skills. At PepsiCo, for instance, divisions whose leaders possessed such qualities outperformed others by 15–20%.

Goleman's theories stemmed partly from the psychological analysis of business leaders by Harvard Business School's **Howard Gardiner**; and also a long-term research project undertaken by Harvard University as a whole which examines the neurobiological basis for defensive and non-rational behavior.

The two professors representing the business school, finance expert **Michael Jensen** and leading thinker on organizational learning **Chris**

Argyris, are using the results to determine why chief executives persist in making decisions that are bound to damage their companies. They have already concluded that the unconscious mechanisms that generate a fight or flight response in threatened animals generate emotionally defensive behavior in humans.

The all-important process to grasp is this: the signal generating fear in humans reaches the amygdala (the part of the brain at the back of the head which is responsible for our emotions) before it reaches the cortex (the front of the brain responsible for rational thought). As a result, humans are driven into impulsive and defensive behavior by their instincts without being aware of it. If we can learn to temper this instinct, our capacity to make effective decisions is therefore transformed.

Goleman stresses that this newly sought "emotional intelligence" is found in two clusters of personal attributes. The first consists of those qualities that help us become more self-aware: emotional self-control, achievement, and adaptability. The second cluster combines those qualities that help us relate better to other people, including the ability to influence, provide effective service, and work well in teams. As he puts it:

> "Better self awareness helps people recognize when they are about to be highjacked by their amygdala, and so become better able to short-circuit the highjack before they find themselves out of control. Empathy allows them to do the same for someone else – picking up the early warning signs of irritation, frustration or anxiety that mark a person at risk from a highjack."

Goleman's espousal of emotional intelligence has inspired a variety of initiatives in both North America and Europe. These include the **Mayer – Savoley** ability model, a diagnostic tool which measures how individuals and their managers identify, use, understand, and manage emotions; and the work of **Victor Dulewicz** and **Malcolm Higgs** of the UK's Henley Management College, which links an individual's emotions and their likely impact on his or her performance with the likely influence of the organization's culture.

EMPOWERMENT

Now somewhat of a hangover from the early 1990s, empowerment – like its contemporary counterpart "employability" – is a classic example of a potentially powerful concept that was turned into meaningless jargon because employers made cosmetic use of it without any real intention of following through on their side of the bargain.

Its main exponent was, and is, Professor **Rosabeth Moss Kanter** of Harvard Business School. Just as Karen Stephenson came to the field of business management from research work as an anthropologist and Danah Zohar as a physicist (see entries below) Moss Kanter first entered the lists as a social scientist.

Associate professor of sociology at Brandeis University before she moved to Harvard in 1973, Moss Kanter's first book, *Men and Women of the Corporation*,[1] was primarily a social study rather than a management guide and won an award in that field rather than in the field of business education.

The issues on which she focused in the research leading up to her best selling volumes *The Change Masters*[2] and *When Giants Learn to Dance*,[3] diversity and equal opportunities in the context of an organization's resistance to change, were framed in a social rather than a commercial context. For example in *Giants*, she describes her notion of equity and fairness in business dealings as

> "related to the new feminist view of morality as encompassing not just analytic 'justness' or 'rightness' in the abstract but also [in] the maintenance of relationships."

Empowerment emerged as a byproduct of this perspective. It envisages managers moving from the role of "boss" to that of "partner" as part of a devolution of responsibility for change and innovation; and individuals taking the initiative in altering standard practice when they see that it is not serving the organization's interests.

Originally developed as a people-oriented strategy to support change initiated from the top, Moss Kanter and other champions of the concept were as keen to stress what empowerment *wasn't* as well as what it was:

"Empowerment does not mean throwing all controls to the wind and allowing people to do whatever they please. Productive empowerment requires discipline and professionalism among staff members, who can be entrusted with greater capacity to act because they have shown that they will handle power responsibly."

Moss Kanter in particular saw empowerment as the centerpiece of a psychological contract that gave staff a greater sense of ownership over their work. In her book *Frontiers of Management*[4] she states:

"I argue that *powerlessness corrupts* ... Those who lack the tools of power and who thus come to feel powerless stifle innovation, over-control others, emphasize rules and behave punitively."

The trouble was that it was introduced at a time when devolution of responsibility to the front line was taking place in the context of delayering and downsizing. Just as "leanness" and business process re-engineering was used as justification to make one half of the workforce redundant, empowerment was used to justify loading the other half with responsibilities it could not undertake for lack of resources – thereby imposing precisely the sense of powerlessness that Moss Kanter sought to remove.

By the time innovation became the prime focus of the board in the late 1990s (see Chapter 3), empowerment had become thoroughly discredited as a management concept. In retrospect, it was remarkably timid in its scope. Hedged in with caveats that suggest that staff should re-interpret management systems rather than challenge or reform them, it has not provided the platform needed for a truly innovative organization to build from.

One of Moss Kanter's colleagues at Harvard, Professor **Chris Argyris**, delivered a devastating attack on the practical implementation of empowerment in *Harvard Business Review* in 1998, including the following comment:

"Managers love empowerment in theory, but the command-and-control model is what they trust and know best. For their part, employees are often ambivalent about empowerment – it is great as long as they are not held personally accountable . . . it remains much like the emperor's new clothes: we praise it loudly in public and ask ourselves why we can't see it.''

In this sense empowerment is an echo of the past but the psychological flaws in how it was implemented still resonate as we enter another period of economic uncertainty.

HOW IDEAS ARE INSPIRED

Our own work in this field, conducted for the UK's Roffey Park Institute, focuses on how recent neuroscientific research feeds into how ideas are 'inspired in individuals on a day-to-day basis.

Through questionnaire-based surveys and follow-up interviews with senior managers from different sectors, we have discovered that their best business ideas are predicated on a triangular relationship between three cognitive processes or factors.

» The first is the presence of a pressing business problem or challenge. This does not have to be in the forefront of the individual's mind when the mental breakthrough occurs – indeed this may act as an impediment. But it needs to be lurking around in the background "bothering" the individual enough for it to act as a backdrop for his or her random reflections.
» The second is a perspective on the problem that will enable the individual to think "out-of-the-box" and see the issue through new eyes. This is shaped by formative influences that stem from a range of interests and activities that extend well beyond work. These include insights picked up from business or personal networking, conferences, courses, private reading, sport, other leisure pursuits, and family life.

   The breakthrough occurs if the individual is able to make connections between previously unrelated fields or concepts – in much the same way as the thinkers and commentators in this section develop new insights into the way organizations work by seeing them from the perspective of an anthropologist, physicist or social scientist.
» The third factor is an environment in which the individual can "drift and dream." Most of the managers we interviewed have a "special

place" where they do their best thinking, although this is often as commonplace as lying in bed, taking a shower, or driving into work. Over time, their subconscious mind associates this place with creative thought, enabling the individual to "fast track" the process with ever more productive results.

We then re-examined common management systems and practices to see whether they support these creative cognitive processes. Once again basing our conclusions on feedback from interviews and questionnaires, we found that a number of key assumptions need to be in place.

» First and foremost is a "no blame" culture in which people are encouraged to take risks and failed experiments are treated as valuable learning along the way.
» Second is a recognition that change or uncertainty, if it is not managed effectively, can lead to "psychological withdrawal," where an individual's ability to think creatively is undermined by stress or distraction; or to "psychological work to rule," where individuals deliberately hold back their best ideas until their position in the company is clearer. Drawing on research by the Mergers and Acquisitions Research Group at Roffey Park, we argue that this is often the reason why mergers fail. The very process of change, if unexplained to the workforce, will undermine the innovative capability that the two partners are seeking to exploit.
» Finally, there is the recognition that the "whole" person is the most valuable to the organization. If the individual is prevented from living a balanced life or if they are unwilling or unable to use personal insights or knowledge in their mainstream work, then the organization is the loser. It is the ability to bring thinking from a non-business discipline or activity to a common corporate problem that most often leads to product or service breakthroughs.

LEADERSHIP AND THE INNOVATIVE INDIVIDUAL

The starting point on leadership and the innovative individual was the move, in the 1980s, away from "transactional" leadership – based on a series of standardized processes undertaken in a stable and unchanging environment – towards "transformational" leadership, where the organization is subject to constant change.

The early exponents of transformational leadership, most notably Professors **Warren Bennis** of the University of Southern California and **Charles Handy** of London Business School, published their work at a time when managing change, pure and simple, was the burning commercial issue. Inspired by a new generation of entrepreneurs like the US's Ben & Jerry and the UK's Anita Roddick, they presupposed that the chief executive's role was to create both the vision and the means to transport the organization towards it.

This notion of a leader's role is still very popular. **Michael Eisner**, the man who turned around the Disney Corporation in the late 1980s, sees the role of the business leader as the man or woman that comes up with the best ideas. In an interview for *Fortune* magazine in 1989, he said that:

> "To me the pursuit of ideas is the only thing that matters. You can always find capable people to do almost everything else."

In a more recent interview for the *Harvard Business Review* in January 2000 he expanded the role to include "nudging" good ideas throughout the organization – but a close examination of the article suggests that, with a few exceptions, the ideas he is nudging are his own.

When the priority shifted from managing change to innovation, the role of the visionary leader started being seen as a liability rather than an asset. Back in the early 1980s, **Marsha Sinetar** of the Massachusetts Institute of Technology had published work suggesting creative entrepreneurs were dictatorial, impulsive, condescending, unable to delegate, and prone to rely on cronies – something all too true of Eisner, who was castigated by the investment community in 1995 for nominating his close friend Michael Ovitz as president of Disney, a costly failure who walked away with a \$100mn handshake without a whiff of opposition from the board.

Sinetar's conclusions were supported by Europe's leading expert on teams, **Meredith Belbin**, who argued in a paper for the business reader *Frontiers of Leadership* that, while "solo" leaders strive for conformity, collect acolytes, and direct subordinates, "team" leaders build on diversity, develop colleagues, and seek talent. He concluded that:

> "[Solo leaders] act as though they have no weaknesses ... The more macho the leader the more submissive the followers tend to be. This effect can be so powerful that the very culture of the company may shift to reflect the solo leader's favored style of working."

The modern view about leadership in an age of innovation is best summed up by **Ronald Heifetz**, director of the Leadership Education Project at Harvard University's John F. Kennedy School of Government. Instead of taking the lead in defining the problems facing the organization and supplying the solutions, Heifetz argues that the "adaptive" leader should free up front-line workers from the constraints of unnecessary rules or regulations, while keeping the organization in a constant state of flux through a continual stream of new goals or challenges.

He compares the process to that regulating a pressure cooker by turning up the heat while simultaneously allowing some of the steam to escape. If the pressure exceeds the cooker's capacity, he argues, the cooker will blow up. However, nothing cooks without *some* heat. Similarly:

> "A leader protects people by managing the rate of change. He or she orients people to new roles and responsibilities by clarifying new roles and responsibilities, framing the challenges they face, helping the organization maintain those norms that must endure and challenge those that need to change."

Note the use of the verbs "orient," "clarify," "frame," and "help." This is a new language for leaders. It presupposes that the impetus for change and innovation is already in place and needs driving effectively through a series of gears rather than the organization being an inert cart that needs to be hitched to a horse provided by the leader. Yet the latest thinking on the subject, outlined by Stanford's **Richard Pascale** and the physicist **Danah Zohar** (see below), suggests that the way truly innovative organizations work is more organic and amebic in nature. Pascale terms them "complex adaptive systems," implying that like biological organisms, innovative organizations change of their own accord.

His analogy was endorsed by **John Mueller**, chief executive of 3M, one of the world's most innovative companies, in a presentation he made to a conference in Prague in 1997. Mueller argued that the characteristics of an "intelligent and networked" organization were not easy to lead in a conventional manner. Intelligent organizations, he stressed, are messy, chaotic, and self-adapting. Staff require new rewards and recognition systems. Management need to stand back and trust:

> "The organization needs to show by its words and deeds that it values people who develop their own processes and performance. They need an opportunity and permission to work on projects that are not defined or necessarily endorsed by management."

NETWORKS AND NETWORKING

Networking has always been a focus of interest in examining how individuals relate to each other in organizations. However the topic has been given a more scientific framework by a young Harvard-educated anthropologist, **Karen Stephenson**.

Inspired by her early twentieth-century predecessor **Margaret Meade**, Stephenson wanted to extend her studies by looking at the intellectual and emotional underpinning of the often unseen interrelationships (what she terms the "hardwiring of the soft assets") of human and knowledge capital in organizations.

Now working at UCLA and Theseus Institute, a business school located in the Sophia Antipolis technology park in the South of France, she argues that social practices used to maintain the cohesion of chimpanzees, gibbons, and other pack animals are mirrored in those practiced by employees in large organizations.

The human equivalent of grooming, according to Stephenson, includes activities such as gossip, small talk, and games-playing. Whether undertaken in a commercial organization or in a social circle, these activities are as important to the group's cohesion as grooming is to the cohesion of the animal pack.

Furthermore, the size of the animal pack seems to be related, among other things, to its collective memory capacity, which is prompted by the ability to remember who reciprocated in the grooming in a similar manner. Stephenson argues that there appears to be a limit to the number of the simultaneous links the human brain can handle and this determines the optimum size of an effective team.

Working in close collaboration with IBM's Advanced Business Unit, Stephenson has used this research to study how networks control the daily life of corporations. She has found that the key figures in these networks, the people who shape the conversation in corridors, play a critical role in bringing about innovative exchanges on a day-to-day basis.

Particularly important are *gatekeepers*, managers who, through a small number of important relationships, link the various parts of the business; and *pulsetakers*, managers whose cross-functional responsibilities cut across all hierarchies and whose web of relationships allows them to know what everyone in the organization is thinking or feeling. Gaining the support of such people, Stephenson says, is critical if the flow of ideas and responses to these is to be sustained and exploited. She explains:

"A good metaphor would be a high security room laced with laser beams and electronic eyes. An innocent gambol across the room will set off a series of alarms. If you are unaware of pre-existing alliances connecting people, you too can unwittingly set off alarms. Harnessing the power of these hidden networks is therefore the key to efficiently guiding innovation and change in a knowledge economy."

Stephenson's theories were used during the sustained economic prosperity of the late 1990s to underpin change management initiatives as varied as relocations and mergers. However, it is worth noting in these more uncertain times that she identified the key roles of gatekeepers and pulsetakers during the downsizing that took place during the last recession, when their intervention in the rumor mill that takes place during job cuts and promotion freezes were used to prevent a hemorrhaging of creative talent.

SPIRITUAL INTELLIGENCE

Danah Zohar, a physicist turned management guru, has built on the concept of emotional intelligence pioneered by Daniel Goleman (see Emotional intelligence above). Over and above the personal attributes Goleman identifies as the hallmark of the effective modern manager, Zohar argues that the neurons which determine our behavior are capable of oscillating in unison – a neuroscientific phenomenon which accounts for our ability to be insightful, creative, and ready to challenge existing ideas and orthodoxies.

People with highly developed spiritual intelligence are, she says, more open to diversity; have a greater tendency to ask "why" and seek fundamental answers; and have the capacity to face and use adversity. They actively seek uncomfortable situations because they recognize that their ability to interpret the environment around them will be enhanced as a result.

Zohar stresses that the new emphasis on examining how the dynamics of the brain shape our intellect and emotions means that effective employers will in the future spend more time helping their less well-adjusted staff break away from the learned behavior that shapes their performance at work. She also believes that most senior managers are trapped in a "Newtonian" view of the world which states that all things are simple, law-abiding, and ultimately controllable – when they should base their perspective on the laws of quantum physics which state that all things are complex, chaotic, and uncertain. As a result, too many management decisions are based on the idea that there is one best way forward rather than the concept that there are many paths to any chosen goal. She explains:

"Apart from the chimpanzee, to whom we are closely related, humans are unique in that when they come into the world, their brains are not wired into any primal behavior. The human brain contains 100,000,000,000 neurons, but by the age of 18 – some say earlier – we're all wired to believe certain things, think certain ways and see the world the way we learned to."

KEY LEARNING POINTS

» New business thinking is emerging from a study of physical and social sciences rather than functional or strategic management theory.

» It stresses that organizations are organic in nature and that, like all organisms, they are complex and adaptive in their dynamics.

» Given this, the kind of black and white thinking and single path orientation that dominated traditional, "Newtonian" ways of looking at business are not very helpful in determining modern business strategy. Assuming and finding ways of coping with paradox, ambiguity, and the idea that there are many equally valid ways from A to B provide a better foundation for managing markets and workers in the twenty-first century.

NOTES

1 Moss Kanter, R. (1997) *Men and Women of the Corporation*. Basic Books, New York.

2 Moss Kanter, R. (1995) *The Change Masters: Corporate Entrepreneurs at Work*. Routledge, London.

3 Moss Kanter, R. (1992) *When Giants Learn to Dance*. Routledge, London.

4 Moss Kanter, R. (1997) *Frontiers of Management*. Harvard Business Press, Boston, MA.

01.07.09

Resources for the

Innovative Individual

» Books
» Articles
» Research

BOOKS

General reading

In addition to those previously mentioned within the chapters:

» Kennedy, C. (2001) *The Next Big Idea: Managing in the Digital Economy*. Random House, New York.

   Kennedy is the leading authority on the work of the world's leading business gurus – she is also author of *Managing with the Gurus*, published by Century. This new book looks at the history of the 'big' idea in business – covering Taylorism, total quality management, business process re-engineering, and emotional intelligence – and looks ahead to the broader social issues companies will have to confront as part of their greater global influence on people's lives. The chapter on how ideas are developed in organizations, which covers new concepts created by Toyota, General Electric, and Shell (among others), is particularly good.

» Kelly, T. with Littman, J. (2001) *The Art of Innovation: Lessons in Creativity from IDEO, America's Leading Design Firm*. Doubleday/Currency Books, New York.

   IDEO is one of the world's leading design firms, responsible for developing, among other things, the Polaroid I-Zone Camera and Crest Toothpaste's Neat Squeeze tube. The founder David Kelly is the epitome of west coast new thinking, and this book, written by his brother Tom, the firm's general manager, stresses that you shouldn't try to imitate the company's rules for success without changing your culture first. Being a design genius is great, he argues, but not at the expense of the team.

» Earle, N. & Keen, P. (2000) *From .com to .profit: Inventing Business Models That Deliver Value and Profit*. Jossey-Bass, San Francisco.

   This book links strategy to the 'big' idea. The point of strategy is to help individuals choose between competing priorities. And according to the authors, the big idea or dream, the company's ambition for the future, can promote a climate of values that helps people make choices for themselves – whether or not to commit to the organization. How people see the future of the organization, individually and collectively, will determine whether it achieves its goals. In this sense, as in politics, the "vision thing" is the key to strategy. Strategy today is nothing without the passion of the people implementing and building on it.

» O'Shea, J. & Madigan, C. (1999) *Dangerous Company: The Consulting Powerhouses and The Businesses They Save and Ruin*. Nicholas Brealey, London.

Though the role of consulting firms as ideas creators is limited to one or two chapters, notably one on the Boston Consulting Group (BCG), this book gives a fabulous inside view of how the big hitters do (or do not) work with their clients. The authors confirm one of our own conclusions – that consultancy–client relationships work best not when the consultancy is forcing its own ideas on the client but when it helps the client place its own concepts and strategies in a broader context or perspective. The debunking of the BCG matrix – dogs, stars, and all – and business process re-engineering, which scored a 70% failure in the organizations in which it was introduced, does more than enough to convince that the big firms should concentrate on analysis and implementation at a micro level and leave big ideas to the academics and the practitioners.

» Langdon, K. (2001) *Smart Things to Know About Decision Making*. Capstone/Wiley.

Langdon is the author of a host of books about practical ideas, including *The 100 Greatest Business Ideas of All Time* and *The 100 Greatest Ideas for Building Your Career*. This latest book covers a number of useful tips for the individual, from formal business trees to backing a hunch. One of the better "how to's" on the market.

» Leonard, D. & Swap, W. (1999) *When Sparks Fly: Igniting Creativity in Groups*. Harvard Business Press, Cambridge, MA.

An extremely useful practical guide to creative exchanges in teams and projects which emphasizes, as we do, that group creativity depends more on managing the creative process as a whole than relying on a few "creatives." It includes plenty of exercises and ground rules that can be used to foster innovative thought, such as the role of "devil's advocates," role playing and scenarios, and provocative physical surroundings.

Books on business from a non-business perspective

In recent years, there has been an outpouring of books that look at the role of the manager, leader, or organization from the perspective of non-business disciplines – whether it be history, philosophy, the physical sciences, or art.

Here is a selection. They all provide the opportunity to look at common business challenges and issues from a different perspective – but bear in mind the caveats we made.

» Adair, J. (1989) *Great Leaders*, Talbot Adair Press. Guildford, UK.
» Roberts, W. (1994) *Victory Secrets of Attila the Hun*, Dell Publishing, Washington DC.
» Morris, T. (1997) *If Aristotle Ran General Motors: The New Soul of Business*, Henry Holt & Co., New York.
» Whitney, J. & Packer, T. (2000) *Power Plays: Shakespeare's Lessons in Leadership and Management*, MacMillan, Basingstoke, UK.
» Krause, D.G. (1995) *Sun Tzu: The Art of War for Executives*, Berkley Publishing Group, New York.
» Belbin, R.M. (1996) *The Coming Shape of the Organisation*, Butterworth-Heinemann, Oxford. (This draws on the advanced communities of insects as an inspiration for group working.)
» von Ghyczy, T., von Oetinger, B., Bassford, C. et al. (2001) *Clausewitz on Strategy: Inspiration and Insight from a Master Strategist*, John Wiley, Chichester, UK.
» Machiavelli, N. *Power: Get It, Use It, Keep It*, Profile Books, London.

JOURNALS

Harvard Business Review

In recent years, this noteworthy journal has focused its attention on issues relating to innovation and ideas development. The best articles include:

» Leonard, D. and Straus, S. (1997) "Putting your company's whole brain to work," *Harvard Business Review*, July-August. (Introduction: "Conflict is essential to innovation. The key is to make the abrasion creative.")
» Amabile, T.M. (1998) "How to kill creativity," Harvard Business Review, September-October. (Introduction: "Answer: Keep doing what you're doing. Or, if you want to spark innovation, rethink how you motivate, reward and assign work to people.")

» Drucker, P.F. (1999) "Managing oneself," Harvard Business Review, March-April. (Introduction: "Success in the knowledge economy comes to those who know themselves – their strengths, their values, and how they best perform.")

» Hansen, M.T., Nohria, N. & Tierney, T. (1999) "What's your strategy for managing knowledge?" Harvard Business Review, March-April. (Introduction: "Some companies automate knowledge management; others rely on their people to share knowledge through more traditional means. Emphasizing the wrong approach – or trying to pursue both at the same time – can quickly undermine your business.")

» Chan Kim, W. & Maubourgne, R. (2000) "Knowing a winning business idea when you see one," Harvard Business Review, September-October. (Introduction: "Identifying which business ideas have real commercial potential is one of the most difficult challenges that executives face. Three tools – to determine utility, price, and business model – can help them invest wisely.")

» Eppinger, S.D. (2001) "Innovation at the speed of information," Harvard Business Review, January. (Introduction: "Developing a new product involves trial and error, but beyond a certain point, redesign becomes wasteful. A practical and proven tool, the Design Structure Matrix, can help streamline the way a company works.")

» Thomke, S. (2001) "Enlightened experimentation: The new imperative for innovation," Harvard Business Review, February. (Introduction: "The high cost of experimentation has long put a damper on companies' attempts to create great new products. But new technologies are making it easier than ever to conduct complex experiments quickly and cheaply.")

» Hayashi, A.M. (2001) "When to trust your gut," Harvard Business Review, February. (Introduction: "How do business executives make crucial decisions? Often by relying on their keen intuitive skills, otherwise known as their 'gut'. But what exactly is gut instinct and how does it work? Scientists have recently uncovered some provocative clues that may change the way you work.")

» Urch Druskat, V. & Wolff, S.B. (2001) "Building the emotional intelligence of groups," Harvard Business Review, March. (Introduction: "By now, most executives have accepted that emotional intelligence is as critical as IQ to an individual's effectiveness. But much of the important work in organisations is done in teams. New research uncovers what emotional intelligence at a group level looks like – and how to achieve it.")

MORE ABOUT THE AUTHORS' RESEARCH

The research highlighted in Chapters 6 and 8 was conducted as part of a long-term program at the UK Roffey Park Institute in Horsham on tracking innovation in the organization. The full findings are highlighted in two reports:

» *Innovation at the Top: Where Directors Get their Ideas From*

and

» *Entering Tiger Country: How Ideas Are Shaped in Organisations*

Both are available from the Publications Department, Roffey Park Institute, Forest Road, Horsham, West Sussex RH12 4TD United Kingdom Tel: 44(0)1293 851644 Fax: 44(0) 1293 851565. www.roffeypark.com; email: info@roffeypark.com

Ten Steps to Fostering the Innovative Individual

1 Focus on the individual first
2 Create a serendipitous working environment
3 Give individuals the "space" to choose their creative ground
4 Allow individuals to make the right connections
5 Recognize and reward successful ideas
6 Let individuals run with their own instincts
7 Provide the right challenge and goals
8 Take advantage of the opportunities opened up by new technology . . .
9 . . . but bear in mind that change on this scale can be threatening
10 Remember that globalism means diversity, not conformity.

1. FOCUS ON THE INDIVIDUAL FIRST

The prevailing wisdom is that, while some individuals are more creative than others, almost all individuals respond more creatively to specific working environments than to others. To gauge how innovative they are likely to be, you have to first focus on how they are likely to respond to the organization in any given situation.

If an individual is likely to feel hostile, suspicious, cynical, or stressed, then it is a sure-fire bet that they will feel either unable or unwilling to use their creative ability on behalf of the organization. If they feel enthusiastic, committed, relaxed, and intellectually engaged, then the chances are they will either contribute their own insights or help shape those of their colleagues.

Sources of stress and alienation cover factors intrinsic to their job, such as work overload, inflexibility in working hours, poor physical work conditions, or a bad relationship with colleagues or the boss. They also include factors intrinsic to the organization, most importantly any prospect of change that is likely to affect the individual's future relationship with the organization, like a prospective merger, alliance, or relocation or, as we enter another period of economic uncertainty, job cuts or promotion freezes.

Tackle these problems first, and the task of fostering the innovative individual becomes immeasurably simpler.

2. CREATE A SERENDIPITOUS WORKING ENVIRONMENT

People create when they feel relaxed. They are at their most relaxed at work when they are engaged in casual social exchanges. So it is not surprising that research by the Massachusetts Institute of Technology and other centers (see Chapter 8) suggests that the most innovative ideas often occur during this banter.

Organizations like British Airways and BMW base their strategies on having working spaces that ensure a rich mix of colleagues – people from other departments, visitors, and senior managers congregate naturally in common social facilities.

This can be fostered still further by recognizing and rewarding what Morgen Hansen of Harvard Business School calls "T-shaped" managers – individuals who freely share ideas and expertise across the organization while remaining committed to their own business unit's performance.

3. GIVE INDIVIDUALS THE "SPACE" TO CHOOSE THEIR CREATIVE GROUND

The mind is constantly processing information even when we are not aware of it. This is what creates the "a-ha!" effect when someone hits upon an idea they have been working away on at the back of their mind for some time.

This often occurs in the most mundane of situations, like while having a shower, driving into work, or settling down to go to sleep. Our own research suggests that once an individual has hit upon the location where creative breakthroughs are most likely to occur, he or she can use that environment as a creative resource as the mind will increasingly associate it with meditation or innovative mental process.

Creating private study areas at work where this kind of mental activity can take place can go part-way towards helping staff become more innovative. However, the more important measure is to provide sufficient flexibility in working patterns to enable each individual to choose where and when they work, within a commonly agreed framework of objectives and targets. One of the most important benefits cited by staff at British Airways working at the company's new headquarters is the ability to choose whether to work at home or on site according to the task in hand.

4. ALLOW INDIVIDUALS TO MAKE THE RIGHT CONNECTIONS

The most important breakthroughs often occur when an individual is able to look at a common business problem from a different perspective. The formative influences that enable them to do this stretch well beyond the office and include insights picked up from professional networking, conferences, business school courses, private reading, leisure activities, and family life.

Effective work – life balance is critical if employees are to have the time and motivation to immerse themselves in these influences.

Help that organizations can provide includes not only encouraging staff to have a life outside work that extends beyond essential family responsibilities, but brokering them into activities like volunteering, sport, and work as local councilors or charitable trustees. Senior managers can also be encouraged to take up roles as non-executive directors.

With all of this in place, the organization should then seek ways to build the insights that staff acquire into their work. One organization we know of encourages employees to build their own leisure activities – such as yachting, football, and even old fashioned pub games like skittles and darts – into activity-based learning linked to their unit's work. Another uses the leisure interests of specific team members, such as birdwatching or Formula One racing, as a source of analogies and metaphors during brainstorm sessions.

5. RECOGNIZE AND REWARD SUCCESSFUL IDEAS

... and realize the difference between the two. Individual recognition is a key motivator. Creativity is the gift of the individual. It cannot be demanded, it can only be encouraged. When it is forthcoming, the organization needs to show it appreciates it.

Ways that firms have chosen to do this include making the individual the centerpiece of the press campaign launching his or her product (Shiseido – see Chapter 7), or awarding anyone who successfully applies for a patent with a plaque, presented at a memorable location to psychologically enhance its value (Nortel Networks – see Chapter 6).

6. LET INDIVIDUALS RUN WITH THEIR OWN INSTINCTS

Accepting that there are individuals who are more innovative than others, those that are, according to Marsha Sinetar of MIT, thrive on freedom in three important areas of life: freedom in the general area of their work and the way in which the work gets done; freedom to ask novel or disturbing questions; and freedom to come up with the solutions to the things they're thinking about (sometimes in the form of what seem to others to be impractical ideas).

Organizations have found different ways to support or encourage this – but the help is mainly confined to top R&D and scientific staff. Hewlett-Packard grants their scientists sabbaticals and encourages them to publish articles on their work. BMW provides cheap laser-molded plastic car components to help R&D staff experiment with wild ideas without incurring unnecessary costs.

This needs to be extended to front-line staff across the organization – but the challenge is convincing them that the organization really means it. Research by Harvard (see Chapter 6) suggests that managers and supervisors have to be explicit and consistent in what they say and what they do. If they say they want staff to experiment in their work but then punish those who fail, employees will draw the inevitable conclusions. This cynicism will be more pronounced among junior staff, who have to prove themselves to colleagues and line managers to gain promotion and who have more to lose if something goes wrong.

7. PROVIDE THE RIGHT CHALLENGE AND GOALS

People need a focus for their creativity. Innovative thinking does not happen in a vacuum. The freedom to experiment and explore is only exciting if it is motivated by a purpose.

Traditional leaders defined the problem and provided the solution, emasculating the creativity of everyone below. Adaptive leaders identify the challenges facing the organization and frame the key questions and answers – and then let their employees find the solutions.

The adaptive leader protects people by managing the rate of change and clarifying their role in the future organization. He or she helps the organization maintain those norms that must endure and challenge those that need to change.

Ricardo Semler, who turned around his father's staid engineering company Semco, feels that staff will only really contribute to his organization's goals on a gray Monday morning if the atmosphere in which they work keeps them feeling excited. Harvard's Ronald Heifetz compares the process to that of regulating a pressure cooker by turning up the heat while simultaneously allowing some of the steam to escape. If the pressure exceeds the cooker's capacity, the cooker can blow up. Nothing, however, cooks without heat.

8. TAKE ADVANTAGE OF THE OPPORTUNITIES OPENED UP BY NEW TECHNOLOGY ...

Email and the Internet open up great opportunities for fostering innovation and creative interchanges across great distances. Research at the Massachusetts Institute of Technology and the University of Manchester in the UK suggests that electronic brainstorming often proves more productive than face-to-face exchanges because less assertive but equally creative members of the group have a greater chance of making their opinions heard.

Our own research suggests that e-mail offers individuals a means of capturing their thoughts more effectively than face-to-face exchanges (where the listener filters out what they don't want to hear) or on paper (where the thinker filters out what he or she doesn't want the world to read).

The new generation of workers, who have been brought up with computers since early childhood, also find it easier to bond with strangers over the Internet, unlike their predecessors who usually require the tacit language of a face-to-face encounter to achieve this kind of bond.

9. ... BUT BEAR IN MIND THAT CHANGE ON THIS SCALE CAN BE THREATENING

HR managers working for the Hong Kong Civil Service in the run-up to the transfer of sovereignty to mainland China examined the reactions of their staff to the upcoming change. They found that civil servants at all levels felt comfortable provided the size of the psychological "box" in which they worked remained the same. If it narrowed, they felt their job was at risk. If it was significantly enlarged, so they could no longer feel the sides, they felt paralyzed by not knowing how far their new discretion to act extended.

To a lesser or greater extent, this is true of employees around the world. Research by Professor Cary Cooper at the University of Manchester's Institute of Technology shows that if you give people who are self-starters and have strong self-esteem the freedom to work in the way that they want to, they will feel inspired. Offer the same opportunity to people who draw security from operating within a consistent framework and they will feel stressed.

British Airways' version of hot-desking at their Waterside head-quarters appealed to staff at the relationship marketing department because they were peripatetic and able to "touch down" at their office between meetings. Administrative staff in the legal and finance departments found it threatening because it gave them no territorial base to work from in a situation where they spent most of the time in the office.

Individuals are individual. According to their age, the technology they are comfortable with, their need for continuity, and the nature of their work, they will respond to change in different ways. Freedom to one person is a threat to another. Staff in one department will need little support. In another, the right training and reassurance will prove essential.

10. REMEMBER THAT GLOBALISM MEANS DIVERSITY, NOT CONFORMITY

The advice applies all the more when the workforce in question is global. Organizations recruiting and training staff for the first time in emerging economies in Eastern Europe, India, and China in the early 1990s found that one of the most enduring problems was that these employees had no understanding of the Western concept of continuous development.

The idea that each individual or work team had the discretion to make changes to work practices on a continuous basis was very threatening. Commentators at the time were quick to point to the effect of local cultures. In China, for example, Confucianism, with its respect for elders and tradition, was seen as an obvious explanation. Some years later, it seems more likely that it is only one factor in a range that includes what style of management employees in the country are used to, the role of the state in the economy, and whether staff are used to collective bargaining or individual negotiations in determining the link between pay and performance – although with the present sensitive state of parts of the world, the different perspectives and assumptions shaped by different religious or spiritual beliefs has suddenly assumed a greater importance.

Professor Gordon Redding, of the international business school Insead in France, makes the very good point that the organizations at the forefront of globalism in the early 1990s had just undergone a management revolution that put a premium on devolution of responsibility, flat structures, and individual pay bargaining. Go back just over a decade to the late 1970s, and the differences between their culture and those of the hierarchical, top-down industries they encountered would not have been that great.

Diversity at the time was seen as something to be molded into conformity, in an effort to provide worldwide services operating to consistent standards. In an age where innovation is at a premium, and political and economic uncertainty a constant, diversity is seen as the organization's biggest asset – something to be tapped, fostered, and celebrated.

Frequently Asked Questions (FAQs)

Q1: Are some people more creative than others?

A: Up to the early 1990s, the answer would have been an unqualified "yes." The research of Marsha Sinetar at the Massachusetts Institute of Technology (see Chapters 2 and 8) and Professors Cary Cooper and Charles Cox at the University of Manchester's Institute of Technology argued that managers who demonstrated certain highly desirable skills, like leadership and entrepreneurism, had distinct personal characteristics that were shaped by their early childhood or formative teenage years.

Recent neuroscientific research at Harvard and at the University of Toronto (see Chapter 8) also suggests that some people are able to make better use of the front right lobal area of their brains which controls those functions that most influence an individual's creativity – like working memory (holding a piece of information while you manipulate it), cognitive skills (looking at a situation in different ways or from a different perspective), and abstract thought.

However, what is still unclear is whether these qualities are genetic, instilled at an early age or subject to influence in the workplace. Organizations as diverse as the Scottish Enterprise Agency, BMW,

British Airways, Kvaerner and North America's Nucor Steel (all profiled in various chapters of this material) have found that groundbreaking ideas emerge from front-line workers who do not have the background or personal characteristics identified by early psychological research in this field. They merely responded to a change in the working environment or company policy.

Meredith Belbin's well-known team-working roles, and how he recommends they are used, probably provide the right answer to this question. He identified certain roles – plant, shaper, resource gatherer – that are more "creative" than others. He also provides diagnostic tools that help individuals identify which roles they are instinctively better suited to.

However, he stresses that it is the "roles" that are more creative, not the "people" performing them. In Belbin's recommended use of them – not always followed or fully understood – he stresses that individuals can *choose* to perform more than one of the roles according to need or their own desired personal development. You may be instinctively suited to playing a support role like company worker or completer/finisher but this does not mean that you cannot aspire to and successfully perform the role of plant or shaper – given the right support by the organization.

Q2: Can you train people to be more creative?

A: The answer to question one above goes a long way to answering this question. You cannot teach people to "be" creative. You can, however, give them a better understanding of what most feeds creative thought (an ability to see things from a different perspective and to draw lessons from different activities or interests) and the environment in which this is most likely to thrive.

You can also provide ground rules and exercises for teams and project-based groups that can help spark new thoughts and avoid the kind of black and white thinking and censorious interventions that cut off a flow of new ideas. These are set out in more detail in Chapter 6.

Q3: What motivates an individual to be creative?

A: It depends how confident they are. People with highly developed entrepreneurial skills thrive best on a high level of freedom, for example to shape the way they work (where and when), to follow up aspects of the work that interest them, and to ask awkward questions that nobody else would.

People used to a more conservative culture or working environment may find this kind of freedom highly threatening (see the case study on British Airways in Chapter 4). They may need more reassurance that they have a license to take risks and more support when they do. But this does not mean that they have less innovative potential – merely that they need to operate from a slightly more well defined "box."

What all but the most unworldly research scientists want is *recognition*. This can and often should involve a financial reward but the more important motivator is public recognition and the sense that the organization values their contribution (see Chapter 4).

Q4: What prevents an individual from being creative?

A: There are many possible blocks to creativity, including stress, an unconducive working environment, an unsupportive line manager or supervisor, uncertainty about the future of the organization or the individual's own role in it, lack of training, a blame culture in which people taking calculated risks are punished or criticized, discomfort with colleagues or fellow team members, and a lack of individual recognition.

Two particular "syndromes" identified by the UK's Roffey Park Institute are "psychological withdrawal," when an individual feels too stressed or inhibited to think creatively; and "psychological work to rule" where an individual deliberately holds back creative ideas as a negotiable asset or for possible use in another firm or a business startup. Both of these most commonly occur during times of organizational change – such as a merger or a major restructure – when a person's future with the organization is uncertain or has not been spelt out properly.

Q5: Can you be creative over the Internet?

A: Yes. In fact there is significant evidence (see Chapter 4) that creative exchanges at a distance using specialist software or a company intranet can prove more fruitful than face-to-face encounters because less assertive participants, who often have equally creative contributions to make, are not crowded out.

Two caveats need to be made. The first is that the creative potential of e-mail or Internet working will depend on the comfort that individuals have with the technology. For example, people less used to no-holds-barred electronic exchanges may need to have had tacit face-to-face contact with the person or people on the other end of the terminal to have developed the trust required, whereas staff who have been surfers from childhood will have little problem bonding virtually.

Excessive company policing of company intranets can also inhibit collective creativity. Innovative exchanges are built on mutual trust and if there is any sense that the exchange is being screened or "tapped" the medium will be degraded as a creative opportunity.

Index